Praise for

"Ever wonder what woul̲ ̲̲̲̲̲̲̲̲̲ ̲̲̲̲ ̲̲̲̲̲̲̲̲̲̲̲̲ feminist Jewish theological minds trained itself on understanding the mystical teachings of the soul of a tzaddik that had manifested itself in this world in her cat? Wonder no more. This piquant, entertaining, yet soulful and spiritual book is the result of that encounter. A book to be savored, like fine chocolate—or catnip."

> —*Rabbi Dr. Aryeh Cohen, Professor of Rabbinic Literature, Ziegler School of Rabbinic Studies, American Jewish University, and author of* Justice in the City

"Rabbi Professor Rachel Adler, brilliant and insightful as always, takes a refreshingly humorous approach to Jewish text and life, reading her feline flatmate as if he is a page of the Talmud or Kabbalah. The breezy and beautiful writing is filled with deep understandings of humanity, Judaism, and life—from one of the greatest Jewish teachers of our time."

> —*Dr. Elana Sztokman, Jewish feminist researcher, activist, author, and two-time winner of the National Jewish Book Award*

"Adler's *Tales of the Holy Mysticat* is an invaluable and tremendous contribution to Jewish thought. What at first may appear to be casual humor quickly reveals itself as profound wisdom teaching from one of the great rabbis of our time. Through beautiful, witty, and precise language, Rabbi Adler instructs readers on many of Judaism's spiritual depths. *Tales of the Holy Mysticat* is a treasure that belongs on the bookshelf next to the great modern Jewish thinkers."

> —*Rabbi Jason Rodich, Congregation Emanu-El, San Francisco*

"A delightful first-person account of life with a great sage and mystical master. The Mysticat has deep Torah wisdom to impart, but only a fine mind like Rabbi Rachel Adler could interpret these arcane yet essential teachings for the rest of us."

—*Rabbi Rachel Timoner, Senior Rabbi, Congregation Beth Elohim, Brooklyn, author of* Breath of Life

"For those as curious as a cat (though you don't need to be a cat lover), this charming, quirky book is destined to become a classic, cherished by those just beginning their Jewish journey as well as those who have been engaged in Jewish study their whole lives. It is an opportunity to explore Judaism with one of the most important Jewish teachers of our time (and her very special cat)."

—*Rabbi Laura Geller, Rabbi Emerita, Temple Emanuel, Beverly Hills, and coauthor of* Getting Good at Getting Older

"An intriguing book. Rachel Adler is always surprising me, in great ways, even when I don't completely understand all the mysticism."

—*Rabbi Naamah Kelman, Dean, Hebrew Union College, Jerusalem, and the first woman ordained in Israel*

"The sweet story of the Mysticat is much more than a book for Jewish cat lovers. I look forward to recommending it to my Introduction to Judaism students as an accessible gateway to the vocabulary and concepts of Jewish mysticism."

—*Rabbi Ruth Adar, Coffee Shop Rabbi and President, East Bay Council of Rabbis*

"A jewel of a book! Not since Eve and the Serpent has there been a connection more beguiling than the one rendered here in word and picture between Rachel Adler and her Mysticat."

—*Rabbi Dr. Lisa Edwards, Rabbi Emerita, Congregation Beth Chayim Chadashim, Los Angeles*

"With her *Tales of the Holy Mysticat*, esteemed feminist theologian Rabbi Rachel Adler has come up with a creative and novel way to introduce readers to Jewish thought, mysticism, history, prayer, rabbinical teachings, customs, practices, and various other aspects of Judaic traditions.

"All of the stories contain an undeniable cleverness, and some are even comical, yet they are filled with deeper meanings and never come off as contrived.

"To say that I gained a new appreciation and insight into the rich diversity and endless complexity of Jewish practices and culture would be an understatement. And you don't even have to be Jewish to likewise gain the same appreciation."

—*Norm Goldman, Bookpleasures.com*

"*Tales of the Holy Mysticat* is a testimony to faith and a way of imparting the messages of Jewish texts and practices from an unusual cat's eye view of spirituality. It is a fun observation of how spiritual growth and reflection can exist even in crabby, difficult personalities such as Dagesh.

"The result is an exploration of Jewish studies that is more accessible than most, teaching not just the foundations of Jewish faith, but the importance in observing the world around us (which may be as close as one's kitty) and translating its actions and insights into the fabric of Jewish traditions and beliefs."

—*D. Donovan, Senior Reviewer,* Midwest Book Review

Tales of the Holy Mysticat

Jewish Wisdom Stories by a Feline Mystic

Reverently Collected by His Humble Assistant

Rachel Adler

Illustrated by David Parkhurst

BANOT PRESS

Contents

Preface:
Why I Wrote This Book

THIS OUTRAGEOUS BOOK BEGAN AS a series of stories I wrote to amuse friends about the idiosyncrasies of Dagesh, my peculiar cat. Over a number of years and a growing body of stories, it became clearer and clearer to me that Dagesh—whom I came to call the Holy Mysticat—was a holy teacher of sorts and that understanding his behavior through the lens of Jewish texts and practice could be a playful way of learning and teaching.

The Holy Mysticat lived with me for eleven years (although for the sake of storytelling, the tales are arranged as if they cover several months). It took both of us a while to adjust to each other's personalities. Truthfully, Dagesh was not the most engaging cat I had ever lived with. He was imperious, obstinate, and crabby, but he radiated a complex spiritual beauty that humbled me. For his part, the Mysticat was fully prepared to dislike and disdain me, yet he apparently saw something in me and ultimately came to love me devotedly, albeit in a grumpy way.

The more I watched the Holy Mysticat, the more he taught me about both the limits of my own Jewish knowledge and the rich possibilities of a playful imagination. The Mysticat was like any knowledgeable Jewish roommate. Thick volumes of Bible, Talmud, and Hebrew or Aramaic lexicons piled on the dining room table seemed homey and inviting to him. He would always be near or on the table when I was learning. He seemed familiar with the rhythms and rituals of an observant Jewish home. But he was also a zealous meditator, a practice at which I am spectacularly unsuccessful. Although Jewish mysticism is not my field of study, its stories and categories seemed to explain some of my roomie's more unusual behaviors.

But I had the power dynamic all wrong: I didn't have a Jewishly knowledgeable cat. Rather, a holy and scholarly feline mystic had *me*, and he regarded me as a gabbai, a sort of secretary-chronicler who also cared for his physical necessities. Historically, a gabbai was a student qua employee who served the great Chasidic rebbes. As a great mystic, the Mysticat was, of course, entitled to this kind of service. But he had expected much higher quality help than me.

First of all, I was not a (male) gabbai but a (female) gabba'it. The Mysticat was a traditionalist and no feminist, though during his years in my home, he learned a grudging respect for female rabbis and scholars. Second, although no gabbai is as learned as his master, no mystic ever had a gabbai as ignorant of Jewish mysticism as I. I am not merely unfamiliar with its texts; I do not comprehend its concepts, even when I can recite the explanations. It's like being tone deaf. I can't even hear it, much less do it. The Mysticat believed he deserved better, and I agree. I can't explain why he got me any more than he could. Third, not only is it untraditional for a gabbai or gabba'it to pursue his or her own scholarly work, the feminist Jewish philosophy and hermeneutics that I produced scandalized and infuriated the Mysticat.

The tales began as a surreal joke. Imagine animal fables in which the moral teacher is not Aesop but a cat. I had no intention of publishing the stories, but my friend the novelist and publisher Maggie Anton was determined. The proposition that she and my scholarly editor, Rabbi Beth Lieberman, suggested to me appealed to my sneaky mind. We would tempt people with these outrageous Mysticat tales and provide appendices so they could get all the learned jokes. Without meaning to, readers would end up adding to their Torah learning. That seemed an appropriate tribute to the Mysticat's own sneakiness, as well as a way to honor the insights he and I had sneaked into one another's awareness. Go ahead, dear reader—see if you can read this book without learning a single damn thing. We give you our blessing.

Acknowledgments

THIS BOOK CAME TO BE because my publisher, Maggie Anton, saw the stories on Facebook and was determined to make a book of them. I am grateful to her for imagining what I would never have imagined myself. I am also grateful to Dave Parkhurst for the lively illustrations depicting the Mysticat and his environment. Dave did meticulous photo research and site visits and then let his amazing imagination run free in the Mysticat's world. The Mysticat himself would have frowned on these depictions because "charm is deceitful and beauty is vain" (Prov. 31:30), but with all respect, the Mysticat could be quite a sourpuss. Special thanks to Rabbi Beth Lieberman, my editor, for shepherding me through not just text editing but also creating the educational materials included in this volume. Not only was she infinitely patient with my grousing about changes in wording, she contributed substantially to the reference materials, especially the glossary and timeline. My talented son, Rabbi Amitai Adler, wrote the reference materials about mysticism and midrash, as well as the lion's share of the timeline. Thank you to almost-rabbi Mira Weller, who also contributed to the glossary. Rabbi Ruth Adar and Muriel Dance, director of the Sandra Caplan Community Bet Din, were kind enough to read the entire manuscript and gave useful feedback.

Many students and colleagues were Facebook fans of the Mysticat and responded, sometimes hilariously, to accounts of his exploits and his philosophy. Sometimes they clarified the Mysticat's reasoning or textual sources for the benefit of the sometimes puzzled assistant to the holy personage. My gratitude and my blessings (such as they are) go to all.

Introduction:
What You Need to Know If You Are Not
a Kabbalist or Talmudist

IF YOU ARE A KABBALIST or Talmudist, read no further. You will get all the jokes and, hopefully, won't be offended by them. If your Jewish knowledge is spottier, which includes most of us, you may want to use the appendices provided in the back of the book. They include the following:

- A short article on the cycle of the Jewish year and its many holidays and fasts
- A short introduction to Jewish mystical literature, which any real Kabbalist will find inadequate
- A short introduction to how Jews read sacred text, which is different from the way other religions read sacred texts
- Short articles explaining the Talmud, midrash, halakhah, and codes, since these are referenced in the tales, sometimes with what some might consider unbecoming levity
- A timeline that lists significant events in Jewish history, when (roughly) various kinds of sacred texts were compiled, when famous people were born or wrote

their reknown works, the various times Jews were massacred (too frequently, alas), and other important dates

- A glossary so that if you don't know if the unfamiliar
word you stumbled on is a holiday, a sacred text, or the
way to say "yeet" in Aramaic, you can be directed to an
explanation

And now, read on and enjoy!

I

The Mysticat Arrives

SPRING 2007

I HAD JUST MOVED INTO a new apartment. I shelved the books, organized my desk, and made the kitchen kosher, but something still seemed to be lacking. This home needed a cat. Online I scrolled through scores of photos from local shelters until the face of one particular cat leapt out at me. It seems crazy to say this but I knew immediately that he was a Jewish cat. Rabbi Robin Podolsky accompanied me to the shelter where I met in person a sizable gray tabby. He was sick, gaunt, and caged, but he retained his *hadrat panim*, the spiritual beauty of face and dignity of mien that mark a great soul. I never did learn the Mysticat's biography. In retrospect, I've since inferred that he learned in a good yeshiva and that while still a promising Mystikitten, some great adept taught him the secret Torah (Torat Nistar). Then some catastrophe drove him onto the streets, and he became "a restless wanderer on the earth—*na v'nad ba-aretz*" (Gen. 4:12). He was wandering in downtown Glendale when he was caught and incarcerated.

Robin and I conveyed him home. We had been cautioned that a cat might prefer to stay quietly in a single small space

until it has become accustomed. But when we opened the crude cardboard carrier in my study, he was immediately at home among the massive Hebrew volumes, purring and rubbing against them as if they were old friends. After an attentive tour of the bookshelves, he went to the door, and as soon as we had opened it, he sallied forth without hesitation to view his new kingdom.

He approved the *mezzuzot* on every doorpost, the meticulously kosher kitchen, the display of silver Shabbat candlesticks, braided beeswax Havdalah candle, spice box, menorah, and more books. The sunlight pouring in everywhere, the broad windowsills perfect for feline recitations of psalms and liturgical poems (piyyutim), the cool glossy wood floors, and the spare but comfortable furnishings all elicited from him cries of astonished pleasure.

Shortly after the Mysticat settled in, he was presented with a fountain placed on the floor, convenient to the low platform where his blue and white bowls for wet and dry cat food sit. The Mysticat meditates on this fountain. After all, the Torah itself is compared to a *maayan*, a fountainhead of living waters, fluid and inexhaustible. Every time the learner comes to drink, the waters are new. Every text can yield new illuminations, no matter how many times it has been studied. Shefa itself, the Kabbalistic terminology for the outpouring of divine influence, suggests fluidity, although its abundance is usually imaged as an outpouring of light. Yet light too can be liquid. During the only times in my life that I later identified as mystical experiences (which happened just twice), the light had the quality of slowly flowing honey.

Tranquilly, the Mysticat reviews his Zohar while the fountain flows and light surrounds him. He is dimly aware of the hum of women at the table, mostly learning Talmud or preparing a chanted Torah reading. And even though the entire notion of women scholars is a shock to his traditionalist sensibilities, occasionally a word, melody, or teaching makes the Mysticat stop and listen, and holy joy floods in. How happy we are—*Ashreinu!* he thinks. How goodly is our portion—*Mah tov chelkeinu!*

4

Shevirat Ha-Kelim

THE *SHULCHAN ARUKH ORACH CHAYYIM* 1:1 exhorts us
to arise in the morning like a lion to do the will of our Creator.
The Holy Mysticat, being more closely related to the lion than I,
finds it easy to obey this dictum. If I am unresponsive and linger
in bed, he leaps onto the bedside table to reenact the Breaking
of the Vessels—Shevirat Ha-Kelim, the cosmic catastrophe
that, according to Lurianic Kabbalah, caused the formation of
the material world. With an inexorable paw, he sweeps everything from the table onto the floor. Galvanized by the series of
deafening crashes, I jump out of bed shouting, "Okay, okay!"

In a manifest proof of divine mercy, I present to the Mysticat
his morning meal. Now he can begin his favorite mitzvah: raising the *nitzotzot*—the sparks of the Divine—from his cat food,
in which, as in all other material things, the embedded energy
must be extricated and released. The Mysticat performs this
liberation of the *nitzotzot* with profound intention—*kavanah*.
I observe it with somewhat less *kavanah*, torn, as usual,
between my fragile impulse to do good (*yetzer ha-tov*) and my
all too robust impulse to do evil (*yetzer ha-ra*).

5

Tefillin

WITH DEEP INTEREST, THE HOLY Mysticat is watching me don the garments of weekday morning prayer. First I
swirl the great tallit over my head and torso. While doing so, I
murmur the blessing (berakha). For this moment, I am under
the wings of the Shekhinah. Then, on go the tefillin. When the
long strap (*retzua*) of the arm piece (*shel yad*) starts to dan-
gle, the Mysticat's *kavanah*, his holy intentionality, catches
fire. God may have placed enmity between the woman and the
serpent (Gen. 3:35), but that enmity is nothing to the state of
war between the snake and the cat. This long, sinuous black
strap perfectly symbolizes for the Mysticat the primeval serpent who is, according to the Talmudic sage Resh Lakish, also
the Satan or Accuser, the Angel of Death, and the *yetzer ha-ra*,
the Impulse To Do Evil (*Bava Batra* 16a).

The Mysticat's own tefillin ritual, therefore, is a spirited
enactment of the cat's triumph over this primal enemy of the
soul. He pounces, wrestles, claws, and bites the representation
of evil, until I remove the mangled enemy from the fray so I can
complete my own tefillin ritual, which began earlier as a much
tamer affair. I wind the long *retzua* on my arm and then place
the *shel rosh* around my head with the *bayyit*, the box hous-
ing the parchments, positioned exactly above where a Hindu

would say my third eye is located, the one that sees into the mystery of things. Finally I return to the arm *retzua*. I make the triple ring on my finger and recite the betrothal verse (Hosea 2:22) that makes me the inconceivable promise that I will know God. Then I make the letter *shin* on my hand to stand for the divine name Shaddai and pray the morning (Shacharit) service.

The Mysticat's tefillin ritual was born out of the tzaddik's inspired ability to seize the holy potentialities continually presenting themselves. Human tefillin are obviously not built for a feline servant of God. These ritual objects require long arms, clever fingers, and opposable thumbs. The Mysticat is rather amused that humans need to dress up to pray instead of relying on our own good velvety fur to absorb the outpouring of divine energy (Shefa). But then, as he recollects, we have no fur; we have nothing but our miserable naked skins that leave us vulnerable to everything and make us look as if we had been flayed, God forbid. No wonder we developed symbolic clothing even for prayer! And occasionally we do stumble upon felicitous and potent symbols that a Mysticat knows best how to use.

You would be mistaken to conclude that ritual and symbol are foreign to the Mysticat. He is drawn to any ritual involving light: contemplating the flames of the Shabbat and Havdalah candles and the branched menorah that represents a tree on fire, in addition to engaging in his own mystic rituals of bathing in light. Song is equally important to his liturgical practice. I have recounted his yowling Tikkun Chatzot at midnight and his joyous and savage cat-verse of *Perek Shirah* that so frequently rises to his lips (Obad. 1:4). He offers up a fervent and melodious Hallel for festivals and a full repertoire of daily prayers and

piyyutim. I have also witnessed his noisy Shevirat Ha-Kelim enactment of the cosmic catastrophe that resulted in the material world.

In addition, the Mysticat will occasionally resort to metaphor, even concerning secular matters. For example, if some well-intentioned fool places before him a tidbit she erroneously supposes might appeal to a fastidious being, such as the jellied broth from gefilte fish, the Mysticat walks a majestic circle around the offending morsel, turns his back to it, and kicks at it with the very gesture he uses to cover what he has deposited in his litter box. His assessment of the unworthy food is all too clear; indeed, the metaphor is coarse, but the Mysticat does not mince words, especially where dinner is concerned.

I am merely a humble disciple, but it seems to me that while the Mysticat *uses* ritual and sometimes metaphor, he is not *tied* to concrete symbols as I am (even literally) tied to my tefillin. The connections that happen in my brain when I engage with holy artifacts come to the Mysticat's brain through his sensitive paws and nose. They convey to him nuanced information far beyond what I can take in, plus all that a powerful mystic holding worlds upon worlds in his head can imbibe and construct.

I, who am no mystic at all, imagine the mind of the Mysticat leaping from branch to branch of the upside down tree of divine emanations—the Tree of Sefirot, whose roots are in heaven. He crouches on the knotty limb of his choice like one of his fiercer kin, soaks in the particular Torah of that place, and moves "higher and higher" (*l'elilah u'l'eilah*), as we say in the special wording of Kaddish for the Days of Awe (Yamim Noraim). And since the roots of that tree are in the heavens (*shamayim*), higher and higher and deeper and deeper are really all the same. Oh, if I could leap like a Mysticat and play in all the worlds of God! But I'm not built for it any more than the Mysticat is built for tefillin. All my mind can do with that wondrous tree is to register that She is a tree of life to those who hold on to Her (Prov. 3:18). So I throw my arms around her, whatever branch or bark I can reach, and I'm not letting go. Ever.

6

The Canine Hora

TODAY ILENE COHEN CAME OVER to learn with me in preparation for her teaching on Parashat Balak (Num. 22–24). She had brought the *Etz Chayim*, some other Torah commentaries, and her Balak, Bil'am, and donkey puppets. She also brought her little dog Chipper. In principle, the Holy Mysticat approves of interspecies tolerance. After all, not everyone can be a cat. He has been fairly gracious to me, but dogs are a delicate issue. The topic first came up recently when my grandson Michael declared that he had a Mystidog. As an acosmicist, the Mysticat had to acknowledge that since he believes the entire creation is part of God, dogs must be as much a part of God as anything else. However, he added, he had never encountered a dog who knew Chumash with Rashi, much less the esoteric literature of Jewish mysticism. A dog might be a part of God, but an aware part of God? A scholar? A mystic? Unlikely.

Today, when Chipper and Ilene appeared at the door, it so happened that the Mysticat was in my bedroom closet engaged in profound meditation. We decided that rather than interrupting his holy activities, we should just close the bedroom door. That way we would not disrupt him with our boisterous Torah study at the dining room table, already piled with lexicons, Mikra'ot Gedolot, and other reference works. Chipper was pleased to encounter Rashi and other commentators. Ilene and I became absorbed in one of the great comic narratives of the Torah—that of the talking donkey. Suddenly we noticed that Chipper had made himself very much at home. The Mysticat, an abstemious ascetic, had partaken only sparingly of his morning meal. Chipper, in the time we were studying, had polished off both wet food and dry food and drunk deeply from the Mysticat's personal water fountain. "I am not a prophet nor the son of a prophet" (Amos 7:14), but I could prophesy with some certainty that if the Mysticat caught Chipper's scent on his dishes and fountain, it would be a bad day for interspecies tolerance.

Happily, Chipper had shown no interest in the living room rug, which would hold scent better than the wood floors. He had made no attempt to resurrect the mousie with which the Mysticat practices the resurrection of the dead (*t'chiat ha-metim*), the miracle at which the prophets Elijah and Elisha were expert (1 Kings 17:17–22; 2 Kings 4:32–35). Chipper probably wouldn't have known step one in the process any more than I do myself. But he did get the point of Numbers 22–23 and observed dryly that the donkey was not the biggest ass in the narrative.

While Ilene collected her books and a sated Chipper thanked me for the hospitality, I embarked on a meticulous purification of the Mysticat's dishes and fountain involving soap and copious hot water. As Ezekiel promises, "I shall sprinkle pure water upon you and you shall be pure" (Ezek. 36:26). After their departure, I refilled the fountain, put fresh food in the dishes, and cautiously opened the bedroom door. The Holy

Mysticat emerged slowly from his afternoon of contemplation. Occasionally he sniffed the floor as if puzzled. He approached his food, changed his mind, and turned away. Like Shimon bar Yochai and his son, he was heading back to the cave (*Shabbat* 33b–34a). But I diverted his attention with a special hors d'oeuvre: tidbits of home-roasted turkey breast. He made a U-turn and accepted a few.

I was neither surprised nor alarmed by his capricious appetite. I knew he would get to his other food later this evening, after he had worked up an appetite performing his watchcat and demon-patrol duties. I did not mention Chipper's visit, and he did not ask. Naturally, if asked point blank, I could not reconcile it with my conscience to dissimulate, but as the English say, "least said, soonest mended."

7

Preparing for Shabbat

DAGESH, THE HOLY MYSTICAT, PREPARES for Shabbat by engaging in pre-rest rest. In this practice, he imitates the first mystics—the *chasidim ha-rishonim*, described in *Berakhot* 5—who used to prepare for an hour each time they prayed and then meditate for an hour after they prayed. As the Gemara notes, this consumed nine hours of the day. The Holy Mysticat outdoes even these pious men. Of course, as I sometimes take the liberty of reminding him, he is free to engage in his holy activities because, like those pious sages, he has a woman to take care of all his material needs. The implications of this critique have never quite penetrated the Mysticat's consciousness, but he wishes all who are preparing, in whatever humble manner, a blessed Shabbat.

8

Commune in Your Hearts (Imru B'levavchem): A Tale of Meditation

THE HOLY MYSTICAT IS RAPTLY contemplating the insides of his eyelids. He prefers this technique for meditation. He performs this spiritual exercise curled up on what is now his office chair underneath a towel. This towel was draped over the chair by his ignorant but well-meaning gabba'it to preserve it from cat fur, but the Mysticat immediately intuited its holy possibilities.

He takes refuge beneath it since as *Eruvin* 100b so accurately observes, one can learn modesty (*tzniut*) from a cat; and, as all good educators know, any moment may become a teachable one. Even more importantly, like Moshe Rabbenu, whose face shone (*karan ohr panav*) after his communications with the Divine (Exod. 34:29–35), the Holy Mysticat in meditation emits an effulgence too bright for human eyes and must therefore veil himself.

Because this practice is carried out in deep silence, it appears to the casual observer that there is nothing on the chair but a wadded-up towel. In this way, the Mysticat achieves *bittul ha-yesh*, the abnegation of his somethingness—an impressive feat for a rather substantial animal! Silence is traditionally a feature of meditation, as we read in the conclusion of the liturgy for the Bedtime Shema: "Commune in your hearts upon your beds and be silent—*Imru b'levavchem al mishkavchem v'domu*" (Ps. 4:5). We, of course, obey this injunction only at night, but the Mysticat is a great believer in going beyond the legal minimum (*lifnim mi-shurat ha-din*). Hence he engages in these devotions evening, morning, and noon (*erev va-voker v'tzohorayim*). Especially *tzohorayim.*

9

The Mysticat and the Mocker

THE NAIVE READER MAY IMAGINE that the Holy Mysticat leads a tranquil existence, punctuated only by prayer, meditation, and simple repasts. But if you read your psalms and your history, you must know that for the last three thousand years or so, the impious have derived entertainment fairly regularly from mocking and harassing·the godly. "Happy is the one who has not sat in the company of scoffers," declares Psalm 1:1. The writer of the massive Psalm 119 plaintively complains, "Although the arrogant mocked me terribly, from your Torah I did not swerve" (Ps. 119:51), but confesses a few verses later, "Rage about the wicked seized me" (Ps. 119:53). Rage seizes the Mysticat as well. Indeed, even as we speak, a mocker afflicts the Holy Mysticat himself.

While the Mysticat is ascending through the spheres, his furry body ensconced in his office chair in front of the sunny floor-to-ceiling window that leads out onto the balcony, a contumacious squirrel leaps onto the Mysticat's own balcony to taunt him. The nature of this squirrel's heresy is unclear. He may be an *oved kochavim*, that is, a pagan, or even an atheist. His mockery begins in the classical mode quoted in Psalm 3:3, "There is no deliverance for him through God!" and proceeds to the traditional jeer, "Where is your God?" (Pss. 42:4, 115:2).

Ultimately the squirrel descends bathetically into the vernacular "Na na na na na!" The Mysticat, who is by no means a pacifist, hurls himself at the glass howling with righteous rage. Going into his hunting crouch, he pounces, shrieking imprecations in Hebrew, Aramaic, and Cat.

To the Mysticat, the squirrel is a manifestation of the Sitra Achra, the dark side, as it were, of the Divine. The Mysticat's most devastating proof text for this moral judgment is an argument from silence. There is a lovely medieval mystical text called *Perek Shirah*. It is based on the belief that the entire cosmos and all its creatures pray, each in its own unique way. Each entity or creature has a biblical verse of its own. The cat, as the Mysticat proudly points out, has a fierce and martial verse from the prophet Obadiah: "Even should you rise as high as eagles, place your nest among the stars, even from there I'll pluck you down, says God" (Obad. 1:4). The Mysticat quotes his verse to the squirrel. But the squirrel has no verse at all! According to the Mysticat, this omission proves that the squirrel is a mocker and denier. That is why he has incurred that most terrible of curses: "May his name and his memory be erased—*Yimach sh'mo v'zikhro.*" Ultimately, says the Mysticat, citing *Shabbat* 30b and *Avodah Zarah* 3b, God Godself will mock the wicked. He who laughs last, laughs best.

10

Postscript to the Mysticat and the Mocker

SOME OF THE MYSTICAT'S READERS might be shocked by his behavior during his encounter with the squirrel, feeling perhaps that the Mysticat was intolerant and did not engage appropriately in interfaith dialogue. I would like to point out that while this accurately describes one aspect of the encounter, the squirrel did not engage in appropriate or reasonable behavior either. Jeering at other people's deities does not demonstrate respect for diversity. In *Avot* 2:14, Rabbi Eliezer advises, "Know how to answer the *apikoros*," or the heretic. The Mysticat's response requires elucidation. As he himself would acknowledge, the Mysticat is zealous for God (a *kana'i*), like Pinchas, whose act on God's behalf in Numbers 25 is best left undescribed (see Rashi on Numbers 25:8). As Rav Hisda cautions in *Sanhedrin* 82a, there is a fine line between zeal and outright murder. I did reassure my readers that this particular heretic is in no danger of becoming a Mysticat hors d'oeuvre: the window glass is thick, and the Mysticat weighs only twelve pounds. If your notion of a tzaddik is a holy teddy bear, the Mysticat is not going to be your cup of tea. For further illumination on this issue, see Rabbi Amitai Adler's responsum on Tzaddikim Who Bite, in which he deals with such figures as the Holy Mysticat and the Kotzker Rebbe.

II

The Mysticat as Thwarted Writer

I AM GRADING PAPERS. THE Holy Mysticat lies near me
on the bed, eyes tightly shut. He is in a deep trance, yet one
paw rests possessively on a pen. The Mysticat's great sorrow
is that he cannot write. He cannot leave behind a record of
the visions and angelic messages communicated to him or even
his own commentaries on sacred texts. Many great mystics did
this for themselves. Rabbi Yosef Karo, codifier of the *Shulchan
Arukh*, recorded conversations in which he was instructed by
a tutelary angel. After his death, these were published as the
Maggid Meisharim. Rabbi Nachman of Breslov had a scribe,
Reb Nosan Sternhartz, who not only transcribed the rebbe's
great work *Likutei Moharan*, but also recorded all he heard of
the rebbe's teachings. Unfortunately I am no Reb Nosan. Not
only am I unable to follow the Mysticat into his trance, even if
the iconography of his vision were vouchsafed to me, I would
not have the smallest inkling of what it meant.

The Mysticat cannot understand what he could have done
to deserve me as a gabba'it. Instead of someone like the disciples extolled by Rabbi Yochanan ben Zakkai in *Pirkei Avot*
(2:10–12); the Ba'al Shem Tov's disciples, Rabbi Yaakov Yosef
of Polnoye or Rabbi Dov Ber of Mezritch, who quote his teachings and teach them to the world; or the aforementioned great

tzaddik Reb Nosan, the Holy Mysticat, in what is surely his final incarnation (*gilgul*), having attained the most perfect form flesh and blood can assume, gets—wait for it—a female Reform rabbi who learns nothing but Gemara and stupid philosophy, most of it by *apikorsim*. Not only is she incapable of getting even the alef-bet of mysticism through her thick head, she sits at her computer writing a book of her own. It is just too much! Surely no truly sensitive soul would blame him for walking over her keyboard every chance he gets. Perhaps this torment is completely unmerited by the recipient and bespeaks divine love and favor (*yesurim shel ahavah*), like the trials of the Suffering Servant of Isaiah 53. Yes, a passage (*sugya*) in *Berakhot* 5a discusses the whole issue. Even the stupid gabba'it must know it.

This gabba'it does know it and is indeed sorry for the thwarted tzaddik. To be unable to communicate the complexities of what one knows, and worse, what one knows about the Holy One—that is a terrible torment indeed! I would never mock a being in such a situation. It would be like mocking the poor or the dead. In her recently completed dissertation, Reb Mimi Feigelson brilliantly explicates *Berakhot* 18b, the very text that establishes this prohibition. I could look for the passage if I were not in this bed grading papers.

At this point, the Mysticat, who has grown into his fullness as a gray tabby of impressive size, stirs and opens his penetrating emerald eyes. I take this opportunity to run the lint roller over the dark blue bed linens on which short gray hairs are liberally scattered. The Mysticat notes my activity, glances at my cropped silver head, and accuses me of shedding. Fortunately,

one of my previous rebbes taught me that when you are pro-
voked but know you should not answer back, the best course of
action is to recite silently ten times the verse "*Netzor leshonkha
me-ra*—Keep your tongue from evil" (Ps. 34:14).

By the time I have finished with the lint roller and the recital,
the Mysticat has relapsed into his meditative state. He looks
innocent and vulnerable and furry. I recall that my students
also looked innocent and vulnerable when turning in their
virgin insights on Franz Rosenzweig, Martin Buber, and other
Jewish thinkers, who may be as opaque to them as the Zohar
is to me. What a dilemma! It is terrible to be unable to pass
on the holy knowledge one has, and it is also hard to struggle
toward what elusive knowledge one is expected to master. And
it is also frightening to sit down at the computer suspended
between what one knows and what one hopes to discover in
the act of writing. As my colleague Rabbi Dr. Tamara Eskenazi
says, "I write to find out what I think." A little compassion all
around would not be a bad thing, I reflect, as I pick up my pen
to resume grading.

12

A Visit to the Vet

THE MYSTICAT WENT FOR A checkup to the vet, but he did not go gently. First, I had to close off all escape routes before he could be induced to enter his carrier, which is for him a *metzar*, a narrow space in which one is trapped, as Psalms 116:3 and 118:5 would have it. The Mysticat also bitterly cites Lamentations 1:3 about the unfortunate Zion: "All her pursuers overtook her in the narrow places—*Kol rodfeiha hisiguha bein ha-metzarim.*" Once he was in, he delivered a heartrending Tachanun. As recommended in Lamentations 2:19, the Mysticat poured out his heart like water. Vainly, I expostulated, reminding him that "you shall preserve your health—*u'shemartem et nafshoteichem*" is an important mitzvah (Deut. 4:15; *Mishneh Torah Hilkhot Deot* 4:1). The Mysticat favored me with an icy glare from within the confines of the carrier.

At the clinic, the Mysticat refused to emerge from the carrier. I had to unscrew all four wing nuts and remove the top to extract him. In vain the vet complimented his extraordinary emerald eyes and the luster of his plushy gray pelt. After the necessary blood work, inoculation, nail trim, and the purchase of quantities of expensive prescription food, the Mysticat was free to depart. "Well," I remarked to him by way of consolation (*nechemta*) as we drove homeward, "you now have an opportunity to *bensch gomel!*" This blessing for salvation from life-threatening danger is one that seldom comes the Mysticat's way. The Mysticat, however, regarded me with boundless contempt from the depths of the carrier. As soon as we reentered the condo and he was released, he disappeared into the closet to meditate on the machinations of the Sitra Achra, the demonic parallel to the holy, and the resulting tribulations of the righteous. Significantly, he emerged promptly and demolished his evening repast. Perhaps the Holy Mysticat holds by *Berakhot* 9b: "One day's trouble is enough for one day—*Daya tza'ara l-'sha'ata.*" He will not brood on vet visits to come.

13

Memories of a World Relinquished

THE HOLY MYSTICAT IS CONTEMPLATING a small container of vivid green cat grass—special for two reasons. One, it requires the blessing *borei p'ri ha-adamah*, "Blessed are You. . . who creates the fruit of the soil." The Mysticat's usual sustenance requires the blessing *she'ha-kol*, through whose word all things exist. This sentiment pleases the Mysticat, but it is general and abstract, while the blessing (berakha) on products of the soil is delightfully concrete. Two, the scent and flavor of juicy grass recall an outside world the Mysticat renounced in favor of an environment conducive to contemplation, prayer, study, and, incidentally, regular meals. The Mysticat now leaves the premises only in a carrier to see the much loathed vet. He does occasionally slip out onto the sunny balcony, but I discourage these ventures lest, in a moment of spiritual ecstasy (*hitlahavut*), the Mysticat might, God forbid, leap off while attempting to levitate. So the green grass I bring him rouses bittersweet memories of a world relinquished.

14

The Holy Mysticat's
Inconsistent Acosmism

THE HOLY MYSTICAT, LIKE SOME other Jewish mystics, embraces an acosmic theology. Acosmic means "there is no cosmos." Such mystics contend that the Lurianic *tzimtzum*, in which God contracted Godself to make room for a cosmos filled with others, was either ineffective or did not occur. Instead, as the first Lubavitscher Rebbe, the Baal Ha-Tanya, said, "*Alz iz Gott*" (God is all that is). Our sense of being distinct, individual selves other than God is merely illusion. The entire Creation is part of God.

What puzzles me is how this belief can coexist with having an ego the size of Texas and a sense of entitlement of matching proportions (and I've seen it in other acosmicists as well). For example, my saintly *chavruta* (friend and study partner) Rabbi RBO has been ministering to the Mysticat in my absence. The other night, she reports, she filled the Mysticat's wet food and dry food dishes, but he sat in front of the dry food meowing angrily. She could not understand why. Then she remembered that the Mysticat is allotted two Feline Greenies atop his dry food. She hastily produced the Greenies, which the Mysticat promptly consumed. His wrath was abated. (The Mysticat's enthusiasm for Feline Greenies is like my enthusiasm for chocolate.)

But if both the Mysticat and his food are part of God, then should not individual desires and preferences be illusory also, as is our sense of separate selfhood? Once the body has the appropriate food for nourishment, shouldn't that be enough? Isn't it inconsistent of the Mysticat to lust for Feline Greenies? This acosmism seems to me to lack consistency.

I myself believe that *tzimtzum* was both effective and vitally necessary. How else would we be able to have relationships with our Divine Other and with all the others around us? How would we appreciate their quirks and their passions? Learning what matters to others and gladly accommodating them whenever possible is one of the very things that enriches us and makes us grow. How would there be a B'rit, or covenant, if there were nothing other than God? I suppose I will never truly be a mystic. The Mysticat himself thinks me hopeless, though well intentioned. As for our future, the Mysticat will continue to yearn for that *unio mystica* in which he dissolves like a drop of water reuniting with the sea, and I will continue to practice my theology of relationship, and we will love each other nevertheless.

A Birthday Present

THE HOLY MYSTICAT THREW UP his entire breakfast in honor of my birthday. Apparently his intention was to give a gift right from the gut, but really, one of his toy mousies would have been prettier, more appropriate, and required far less cleanup. I suppose the personality of the mystic is calibrated toward excess. As William Blake says in his proverbs in *The Marriage of Heaven and Hell*, "The road of excess leads to the palace of wisdom." True, but the road is hard on the seeker, not to mention those who must accompany him on his journey.

16

The Blessing of Renewed Life: A Yamim Noraim Tale

AT SEVEN IN THE MORNING of Erev Yom Kippur, I found the Holy Mysticat sitting disconsolate beside his fountain. Not a drop of water was coming out. I took the fountain apart and cleaned it thoroughly, searching for whatever might be impeding its functioning. The Mysticat watched anxiously. Neither of us was able to perform miracles like the prophets Elijah and Elisha. The motor was dead and it stayed dead. A chilling omen for beginning a new year! At the very time when we implore the Holy One, "Remember us to life—*Zokhreynu l'chayyim*," the Holy Mysticat's personal wellspring of blessing, source of the life-giving element, had run dry.

Obviously this crisis trumped my other errands. I was at Petco the moment its doors opened, shelling out for a new fountain. I rushed home, washed and assembled it, and watched the evil omen turned to good as a mighty stream of water poured down. As Psalm 30 says, "You have turned my mourning into dancing—*Hafachta mispedi l'machol li*."

The Mysticat rejoiced, but, in an abundance of caution, he continued to perform his own ritual for calling on the Giver of Life, which he does, not just until Simchat Torah, when inscriptions in the Book of Life become final, but throughout the year.

This ritual is the Mysticat's enactment of the resurrection of the dead (*t'chiat ha-metim*), with the assistance of his mousie. The mousie, a repulsive object, is a furry stuffed toy about the size of a small rat. The Mysticat pounces, seizes the mousie in needle-sharp teeth, tosses it into the air, drops it, and bats it with an unrelenting paw so that it skids along the polished floor. This process is repeated until both mousie and Mysticat lie inert. After a while, the Mysticat rises renewed and, in a splendid example of *imitatio Dei* available to only prophets and such tzaddikim, he resurrects the mousie so he can kill it again.

The theological implications of this ritual have always been rather troubling to me. Yes, God is the king who puts to death and brings alive (*melekh meimit u'm'chayeh*), but I would like to believe this process is not merely for divine amusement. I also would like to believe that the purpose is renewed life rather than a new opportunity for death-dealing. Sometimes I really wonder about the Mysticat, *shlita*.

The ritual also reflects the Mysticat's belief in *gilgul neshamot*, the transmigration of souls. The Mysticat believes that in his previous life, he was a human Kabbalist and was rewarded for his piety by being reincarnated as the highest life form made of flesh and blood: a cat. In his present form, he is served by a faithful gabba'it, who, while not a mystic, is at least not a total ignoramus (*am-ha-aretz*). His simple surroundings are clean and abound in *s'farim*, holy books, whose holiness the Mysticat takes into himself by lying on them to absorb their textual content. (I myself covet this ability more than any of the Mysticat's other powers, but alas, the only way I can learn Torah is to pound it into my head with multiple repetitions.)

In this humble domicile the Mysticat grants audiences to the many rabbis, scholars, and rabbinical students who visit to honor him and seek his blessing. Some he blesses. Some he bites. Some receive both acknowledgments. It goes without saying that the Mysticat's blessing powerfully confers renewed life. Just look at his mousie.

17

Mysticat Miracles

TODAY THE HOLY MYSTICAT ACHIEVED two minor miracles.

The first is that although I would have sworn he moved from the bedroom directly into the study, I found his breakfast had been consumed.

The second occurred during the Mysticat's *bittul ha-yesh* practice. As I understand it—and my understanding is pretty dim—*bittul ha-yesh* teaches the mystic that this self, with its needs, vanities, and sense of importance, is not just insignificant but illusory. When the mystic sweeps away this illusion, he grasps what is truly important: he is a tiny fragment of God whose job is to join with other such tiny fragments to help reassemble the divine integrity that was shattered in the cosmic catastrophe known as Shevirat Ha-Kelim, the Breaking of the Vessels.

He so spectacularly abnegated his somethingness during his protracted *bittul ha-yesh* exercises under the towel on the big chair in the study that a visitor very nearly sat on him. Happily I alerted her in time, before the Mysticat's *kavanah* was seriously disrupted.

18

A Winter's Mysticat Tale

IT IS THIRTY-NINE DEGREES FAHRENHEIT in Los Angeles. To those of you in truly frigid regions, that may not sound bad. Indeed, when I lived in Minneapolis and the temperature went up to thirty-nine, we celebrated by going out for ice cream. But here thirty-nine degrees is, well, brisk. Even the Holy Mysticat has been affected by the weather. I finally turned on the heat two days after the Mysticat took the extreme step of davening morning prayers (Shacharit) in the closet, despite the dictum of Rabbi Chiyya bar Abba that one should never pray in a room without windows (*Berakhot* 31a, 34b). Until I turned on the heat, the Mysticat emerged from the closet for only meals and the night, when he actually got under the covers with me. I take this as an indication that the Mysticat either was born or has long resided in the warmer regions, although I do not know his origins.

The Mysticat's usual morning prayer practice is to move from place to place for the various parts of the Shacharit service. He begins the morning blessings in the gray glimmerings of predawn at the bedroom window. For P'sukei D'Zimra, the psalms of praise recited to the King who dwells *b'room olam* (in the heights of the universe), the Mysticat mirrors his Creator by ascending as high as possible. His melodious chant issues from atop the refrigerator, reminding the listener of the lovely nineteenth-century African American spiritual, "Over my head, I hear music in the air / There must be a God somewhere." He recites his Shema at the dining room window, in coordination with the full rising of the sun, just like the *vatikin*, the most ancient mystics, according to Rabbi Yochanan (*Berakhot* 9b). He stands for his Amidah, facing east in the living room.

Perhaps we are urged to pray near windows so that the world full of light and splendor with which God gifted us is revealed, and we are moved to praise its wonder and beauty. Now that the apartment offers more tolerable areas other than the closet, the Mysticat sits on the dining room's broad windowsill, meditating on the cold. Maybe it will snow, he thinks. It has not snowed in Los Angeles since 1962. Of course it snowed in the San Bernardino mountains the other day, and snow was predicted for Palm Springs, but not here. How fine it would be to sit at the window watching white flakes fall, reciting from Psalm 147, "[God] pours forth snow like fleece, / scatters frost like ash. / He flings His ice like bread crumbs. / In the face of His cold who can endure?" (Robert Alter's *The Hebrew Bible: A Translation with Commentary*). For that, the Mysticat would relocate from atop the refrigerator. But it has not happened yet. Indeed, since I began writing, the temperature has risen to forty-three degrees. The Mysticat, his prayers long completed, has curled up on the sofa. He is raptly meditating on the inside of his eyelids, lying strategically under the vent through which the blessed heat is descending. Hallelujah.

19

Apology to the Holy Mysticat

I PUT IN THE SECOND of two fourteen-hour days of writing, fell into bed too exhausted to eat dinner, and was awakened at six in the morning by the Holy Mysticat's customary and energetic reenactment of the Breaking of the Vessels (Shevirat Ha-Kelim), the primordial catastrophe that produced the material world. I was so tired and cross that I yelled at him really loudly. Insulted, he withdrew. I tried to go back to sleep, but my conscience would not permit it, so after my morning ablutions, I prepared the Mysticat's breakfast and tried to make shalom. By that time the Mysticat was in deep meditation beneath his towel and spurned both breakfast and me.

One of my errands, consequently, was to visit Petco. On my return I apologized again and presented my peace offerings: a new container of cat grass and three flavors of Feline Greenies. The Mysticat, mollified, accepted a Greenie and a taste of cat grass. Also, like the courteous angels who accepted Avraham's hospitality in Genesis 18, he had caused his breakfast to disappear so as not to hurt my feelings (see Rashi on this point).

I must admit that the morning Shevirat Ha-Kelim reenactment is my least favorite of the Mysticat's rituals, and I sense that the Mysticat is not unaware of this. His indifference is puzzling. I would have thought an acosmicist would be more empathic. Perhaps having an acosmicist's belief that the self and other are really one, and knowing that the Shevirat Ha-Kelim ritual is deeply meaningful to him, he assumes that in actuality it is deeply meaningful to me as well, and my yelling was simply a manifestation of the Sitra Achra, the dark side of the Divine nature. It is certainly difficult to convey to an acosmicist that you feel discomfort with something when he does not. It reminds me of my Aunt Minnie, who used to admonish her husband, "Better put on your sweater, Joe. I'm cold."

20

Bikkur Cholim Kitty

BIKKUR CHOLIM, VISITING THE SICK, is a great mitzvah and is listed in *Mishnah Peah* 1:1 as one of the mitzvot
whose reward is limitless. The Holy Mysticat does not serve his
Creator for reward, but he zealously observes this mitzvah for
other reasons. I am currently down with an upper respiratory
infection, and the Holy Mysticat has changed his routine so he
can be with me. The sickbed is a holy site, for the Shekhinah
rests above it (*Nedarim* 40a). For this reason (and so as not
to loom over the patient), the visitor ought to seat himself on
a level with the sufferer. The Holy Mysticat therefore begins
his visits by reclining on my upper chest nose to nose with me.
This inspires a moving I-Thou moment. However, despite the
fact that this feline servant of God is exercising special healing
powers, fifteen and a half solid pounds of cat, directly over the
site of infection, is difficult to tolerate.

Even an ordinary visitor takes away one-sixtieth of the
invalid's distress, and the Holy Mysticat can well exceed that
calculus. The coughing seems to disrupt his *kavanah*, however, so after a few prayers for healing, the Mysticat dismounts
and curls up beside me. He closes his eyes and begins silently
to recite psalms, an efficacious practice at a sickbed. He can
remain thus occupied, eyes shut and motionless, for awesome

amounts of time. Of course, he has 150 psalms to work with, some of them very lengthy. Psalm 119, for example, is an eight-fold alphabetical acrostic (an important fact to remember when volunteering to memorize psalms). This makes the Mysticat's feat impressive indeed.

Those whose memory skills are less powerful than the Mysticat's should keep in mind that simply to sit with the sick, even without speaking, is its own mitzvah. The Mysticat is a creature of few words, but his benign presence is reassuring. Neither should anyone be surprised that so holy a being would attend to me, for Abaye teaches that even a great person should visit a humble one (*Nedarim* 39b). The Mysticat has shown extraordinary consideration during my illness. To not disturb my rest, he has been praying his Midnight Lament (Tikkun Chatzot) in subdued murmurs rather than his customary yowls.

Visiting the sick is also special to the Mysticat because it provides an opportunity to imitate God, who visited Avraham in Genesis 18:1 when our ancestor was recovering from his circumcision (*Sotah* 14a). Bikkur Cholim is an outpouring of pure *chesed*, loving-kindness. I am fortunate to have a tzaddik to visit me and a tzadeket, my *chavruta* Rabbi RBO, to bring me food and medicine so I do not need to go out for anything. Yesterday Reb Mimi Feigelson taught my liturgy class when I had no voice to teach with, and we all learned Torah that I could not have taught. I am surrounded by *chesed*. How can I fail to recover rapidly?

21

Further Adventures of the Bikkur Cholim Kitty

I AM FORTUNATE THAT THE Holy Mysticat has a powerful gift for healing since he is unfortunate enough to have a gabba'it who is a magnet for bacteria. The little beasties always head straight for my respiratory system, which is usually followed by a major asthma episode. The Mysticat's custom (minhag) is to curl up on the ceramic stovetop next to the counter where the nebulizer is plugged in. He watches benignly as I sit there sucking in the potent chemical mist that will make my bronchi reopen for business and the rest of my body shake for hours afterward.

Once I totter back to bed, the Mysticat takes a more active role. He leaps up to the foot of the bed and marches purposefully over my supine form until he is nose to nose with me. Then he lies down directly on top of me while praying for my healing, as both Elijah and Elisha do as they miraculously revive the dead (1 Kings 17:21; 2 Kings 4:14).

The Holy Mysticat is both patient and persistent. He reclines his solid fifteen and a half pounds heavily over the afflicted lungs, sending up wholehearted entreaties in a rumbling purr.

Finally, depleted but devoted, he retires to his round velvet bed beside me, closes his eyes (presumably to aid concentration), and silently recites all 150 psalms from memory. He does not move a muscle for hours. Surely I am singularly blessed to have at my bedside a visitor who puts such effort into the mitzvah of visiting the sick!

22

Divine Providence

THE HOLY MYSTICAT WAS NOW ill himself, having had
dental surgery a few days ago. The vet handed me a bottle of
pain pills and a supply of liquid antibiotics to be administered
twice daily with food. Unfortunately, each time I attempted to
administer the drugs, the Mysticat and I had a major theological argument. The Mysticat declared his intention of relying
solely on Divine Providence (*siyyata di-shmaya*) and refused
the drugs. I cited multiple sources to him. His argument was
that the liturgy calls God "Healer of the sick" in the second
blessing of the Amidah and in a separate blessing of the weekday Amidah. In Exodus 15:26, God declares, "I YHWH am your
healer." In Numbers 12:13, Moses pleads on Miriam's behalf,
"Please God, heal her." Jeremiah says to God, "Heal me and I
shall be healed" (Jer. 17:14), which is the reference the weekday Amidah picks up. In response, I contend that Jewish law
makes a strong case for skilled intervention. Exodus 21:19
describes the damages someone must pay for injuring another
and declares, "The injured must pay for the victim's time when
unable to work and the costs of the cure" (*v'rapo yirapeh*).
The rabbis rely on this verse for two of the five kinds of damages (*tashlumei nezek*) for which an injurer is liable (*Mishnah
Bava Kamma* 1:4; *Bava Kamma* 8, a.k.a. *Perek HaChovel*).

That Exodus verse is also cited as proof that physicians are permitted to engage in healing (*Bava Kamma* 85a). None of the rabbis in this discussion suggest that a sick or injured party have recourse to divine providence alone. They assume the injured or sick will and should call the doctor.

Making a sustained argument was proving difficult because the Mysticat kept trotting away and secluding himself in the closet. Kneeling and sticking my head inside the closet, I also referred to the discussion of risk and randomness in *Shabbat* 32a. I particularly pointed out to the Mysticat the words of caution of Rabbi Yannai, "One should never stand in a place of danger and say that a miracle will be done for him. The miracle might not happen."

Still on my protesting knees, I quoted him Deuteronomy 4:9 and 4:15 on the mitzvah of protecting one's own health. I reminded him that the great Maimonides was both a legal scholar and a doctor. He viewed his skill as an instrument of divine providence. Pressing my advantage, I accused the Mysticat of a destructive literalism. Confident that I had won the disputation, I reached in, picked up the Mysticat, and inserted a syringe of antibiotics into his mouth. The Mysticat bit me and fled into the recesses of the closet, dribbling antibiotic onto the floor as he did so.

I protested that violence is not a valid argument. The Mysticat retorted that coercion is not a valid argument either. Since then, the household has been a scene of battle twice a day. In between times, the Mysticat seems to hold no grudge. He settles down beside me companionably to meditate on the Zohar. I think the fragments of pain pills that have gotten past his defense system have had some effect. I devoutly wish it were possible to reason with a mystic and am fervently thankful that the medication is close to finished.

23

A Birthday Tradition

AGAIN, AS HE DID LAST year and the year before, the Holy Mysticat threw up in honor of my birthday. Regurgitation is now a birthday tradition, though I am still perplexed about its significance. Presumably, the Mysticat wished to offer a gift straight from the gut, so to speak. Certainly the copiousness of the donation demonstrates effort. I give him full credit for that. Nevertheless, I wish he had consulted me about my preferences. A spare toy mousie or brightly colored hair elastic would have been much more to my taste. One would think he would have noticed last year and the previous year that my acknowledgments were rather minimal and restrained. I am not sure if his mind was on Higher Things or whether this is just the garden-variety obliviousness that afflicts certain very traditionally socialized males. In any case, I thank my other friends for more aesthetically pleasing birthday greetings.

24

The Mysticat Offended

THIS AFTERNOON I PUT ON a pot of leek and potato soup
with dill for my friend RBO, who is convalescing. The Holy
Mysticat became a little too interested in the preparations—or
so I surmise—because I stepped back from the counter and
heard an unearthly howl. Apparently I had stepped on a paw
or tail or some other portion of feline anatomy. Of course, I
apologized profusely and offered a cat treat in compensation.
The Mysticat responded with scathing comments concerning
Clumsy Oafs Who Tread on Holy Creatures and Then Try to
Obtain *Mechilah* (pardon) through Vulgar Bribery, instead
of what the twelfth-century German mystics were known to
have done—Confessions and Penitential Rolling Naked in the
Snow. I pointed out that we do not have snow in Los Angeles.
Nevertheless, he left the treat in the middle of the living room
floor to make a statement and retired to his meditations.
Perhaps he will soften when it is time for Shabbat dinner. When
we are visited by the two Shabbat angels (*Shabbat* 199b), we
want them to find peace and goodwill here. We certainly do not
want them to find quarreling and anger. Or, Heaven forbid, the

evil angel will say, "May it be just like this next week." Shabbat Shalom and Chanukah Sameach to all.

25

No Food, No Torah
(Im Ain Kemach, Ain Torah)

TODAY THE HOLY MYSTICAT RELUCTANTLY made one
of his periodic visits to the vet so his razor-sharp nails could
be clipped and I could replenish the household supplies of wet
and dry food. He had many objections to this outing. First,
today is Rosh Chodesh, the New Moon of the month of Adar.
We are told that "When Adar comes in, we should increase our
joy—*Mi-she nichnas Adar, marbim b'simcha*" (*Ta'anit* 29a).
A visit to the vet, however, decreases joy. Second, the whole
expedition would result in *bittul Torah*, a waste of time that
should have been devoted to Torah study. Third, the Mysticat
argued, his sharp claws were necessary to keep the mazikin,
the demons, at bay. And fourth, a great tzaddik ought to be able
to delegate grocery shopping to his gabba'it. After all, what was
he paying me for?

I respectfully pointed out that I would experience an
increase in joy if he did not scratch me (accidentally, I'm sure,
but still drawing blood, and what about "You shall not stand

idly by your neighbor's blood—*Lo ta'amod al dam rei'ekha*"
(Lev. 10:16). Second, I reminded the Mysticat that he had many
texts committed to memory and could easily occupy himself
with them on his journey. If he would go over tractate Megillah
in anticipation of Purim, I suggested, he might find that it
raised his spirits. Third, the Holy Mysticat is so well versed
in the incantations that vaporize demons that he need never
lift a paw. Finally, I reminded the tzaddik, he does not exactly
pay me, although I am sure I acquire much merit (*z'khut*) by
serving as his gabba'it. We did need the food, for "If there is
no food, there can be no Torah—*Im ain kemach, ain Torah*"
(Pirkei Avot 3:17), and it would be thoughtful of the Mysticat
if we could get his nails clipped at the same time. *Teku*: the
debate stood without resolution in either direction.

The Mysticat and I then went about our business, but while
he was otherwise engaged, I got out the cat carrier and stealth-
ily closed the bedroom door. I am getting too old to lie on the
floor to extract the Mysticat from under the bed. Strolling by,
the Mysticat perceived the carrier, dived under his towel in the
study, and immersed himself passionately in his *bittul ha-yesh*
exercises, in which the mystic attempts to abnegate his somethingness and reduce himself to nothing. Only a faint sugges-
tion of somethingness was ascertainable under the towel, but
at the appointed hour, I unfairly used the advantages of my size
and musculature to transfer the tzaddik to the carrier.

I sincerely hope his many colorful imprecations in Hebrew,
Aramaic, Yiddish, and Cat will remain unfulfilled, despite the
maxim "The righteous one decrees and the Holy One fulfills
it—*Tzaddik gozer v' ha-kadosh barukh hu mekayem*" (Shabbat

59b), because—citing one favorite Yiddish curse as example—I would not like to own a thousand-room hotel and drop dead in every room. For one thing, being a gabba'it is hard enough without going into the hospitality industry, for which I have absolutely no aptitude, and furthermore, dropping dead just once seems to me entirely sufficient.

The less said about our outing, the better. Once home, the Mysticat retired to sulk in the closet until Shabbat candle lighting. Rosh Chodesh was over, but it would be the month of Adar for another twenty-eight days: plenty of time to get his joy on, I reminded the holy creature. "Huh," he sniffed. I did notice, however, that he consumed a more than adequate Shabbat dinner.

26

Incommunicado

THE HOLY MYSTICAT WAS INCOMMUNICADO most of the day. I arose early this morning, well before one can distinguish between blue and white, which, according to an opinion in the Mishnah, is the criterion for when it is light enough to recite the morning Shema (*Mishnah Berakhot* 1:2). After hasty ablutions, I went to dress, after which I was planning to feed the Mysticat. But the closet light bulb had burned out, and locating appropriate clothing took more time than usual. When I emerged and began preparing the Mysticat's customary repast, the tzaddik did not materialize to supervise as he usually does. I called him but he did not respond. Silent but palpable disapproval chilled the atmosphere.

Apparently the Mysticat believed I had been dilatory in my duty of serving a Torah scholar (*shimush chachamim*). But where was he? Surely he had recited Shema by that time. Like the *vatikim*, the ancient mystics referenced in the Talmud (according to Rabbi Yochanan, *Berakhot* 9b), the Holy Mysticat times his Shema to coincide exactly with the sunrise. When I finally located him, he had, in lieu of breakfast, commenced his *bittul ha-yesh* practice. As I understand it—and my understanding is pretty dim—the goal of *bittul ha-yesh* is the abnegation of one's somethingness.

The Mysticat was doing just that with remarkable efficiency in the large armchair in the study. Under the towel that had been draped over it in a futile attempt to save the upholstery from cat hair, only the faintest outline of a feline form could be discerned. I patted this lump gently and informed it that breakfast was served, but, of course, from the Mysticat's perspective in his present exalted state, breakfast was equally illusory, so I said a courteous farewell and went off to work. When I returned home some hours later, the Mysticat's breakfast had vanished. Either that or it had always been illusory, and I had just realized that fact. The Mysticat himself appeared quietly while I was annotating some papers and graciously received my apologies for the irregularities of the morning. He looked on sociably while I prepared and served his dinner.

27

Bed Mice

AT NIGHT, BEFORE SAYING THE Bedtime Shema, the Holy Mysticat indulges in the energetic pursuit of bed mice. Bed mice are a mysterious and elusive species of rodent. They are akin to mazikin, though they are three-dimensional rather than two-dimensional. You see them under quilts or duvets. An odd coincidence is that they manifest themselves only when human beings are in the bed. They wiggle enticingly. The cat leaps to spring on them. A swift paw can trap one in a nanosecond, but when the Holy Mysticat tries to take a bite, all he gets is a mouthful of down-stuffed cotton. The diabolical beastie just skitters away and reappears a few inches away. Again the cat pounces, the creature firmly captured under a paw, and then it slides out from under. Feline legend has it that bed mice have *ta'am Gan Eiden*, the flavor of the Garden of Eden—like chicken but even tastier. The chase is stimulating but tiring.

I suppose I have my own bed mice, glimmering awarenesses of things I can never firmly grasp. They remain for me something more than mere beliefs or opinions but less than what I can demonstrate through reason or produce to be tested and quantified. I don't know quite what they are, but I know they are there, and I am sure they have the flavor of Paradise.

A quick prayer, and the Mysticat, eyes tightly shut, dreams of bed mice and *Gan Eiden* until he rises at midnight to recite Tikkun Chatzot together with other mourners of a broken world.

28

The Mystery of Pesach

AFTER THE MINCHA SERVICE AND shortly before sundown, extending into the liminal time of twilight, the third meal of Shabbat, *se'udah shlishit*, is served. In contrast to the Shabbat evening meal, whose theme is creation, and Shabbat lunch, whose theme is revelation, the theme of the third meal is redemption and the future. Its mood is quiet and contemplative, and the music sung at the Shabbat table is filled with longing. Some Chasidim claimed that their rebbes had the spiritual power to transcend time and space to partake of this holy meal in heaven (*se'udah shlishit ba'Shamayim*). Of course, the Holy Mysticat possesses this power.

I am heading to Chicago for Pesach, and my saintly *chavruta* Rabbi RBO is tending to the spiritual and material needs of the Mysticat. I am sure she will join him when, as is his custom, he partakes of *se'udah shlishit ba'Shamayim*. As for the *chag*, or festival, the Mysticat does not require sedarim, although he observes tolerantly when I make them at home.

The truth is the Mysticat does not really comprehend the central transformation of Pesach: from slavery to freedom. *You cannot enslave a cat.* You can abuse or kill a cat, but no one has ever succeeded in enslaving a cat. The Mysticat remembers being homeless, flea-infested, and desperately hungry, but his will has never bowed to the will of another. I have read that researchers have never achieved an accurate assessment of feline intelligence because, while dogs, rats, and monkeys will perform actions over and over for small rewards, a cat will perform once or twice, if the reward is sufficiently alluring or the problem sufficiently interesting. After that the cat will simply walk away.

So the Mysticat cannot understand a basic fact about humans: their enslavability. But the Mysticat knows there are more things in heaven and earth than are dreamt of in his philosophy. He does not aspire to tear the veils from every mystery. He sees that we emerge from the seder feeling free. Free is good. The Mysticat rejoices for us and wishes us all a *chag kasher v' sameach.*

29

The Mysticat Ponders the Month of Tammuz

YESTERDAY THE HOLY MYSTICAT CELEBRATED Rosh Chodesh Tammuz with a divided heart. Certainly, any new moon is a blessed occasion. The Mysticat, a mighty singer, loves the Hallel psalms. But he is deeply ambivalent about this month. Tammuz and the month of Av, which follows it, are particularly pleasing to a creature who luxuriates in warmth and light. In these months, the Mysticat abandons his office chair and meditates at the foot of the floor-to-ceiling window looking out onto the balcony. The text he most often calls to mind is Rav's description of the World to Come—Olam Ha-Ba—in *Berakhot* 17a: "In the World to Come there is no eating nor drinking nor propagation nor business nor jealousy nor hatred nor competition, but rather, the righteous sit with their crowns on their heads and bask in the radiance of God's indwelling Presence, Shekhinah" (*v'nehenin b'ziv ha-Shekhinah*). Stretched out to an impressive length parallel to the window, enveloped in the hot, golden light of summer, the Mysticat envisions melting into this future radiance.

Less than three weeks into Tammuz, however, the mood of the month turns tragic with the fast of the Seventeenth of Tammuz. *Mishnah Ta'anit* 4:6 lists five catastrophes on this date: (1) Moses smashed the first two tablets of the law, (2) the daily offering ceased to be brought, (3) the walls of Jerusalem were breached, leading to the conquest of the city and the destruction of the Temple, (4) during the Bar Kochba rebellion, the Roman military leader Apostomus burned a Torah scroll, and (5) an idol was set up in the holy precincts. The Seventeenth of Tammuz inaugurates the *drei vokhen,* the three weeks of mourning that culminate in Tisha B'Av, the Black Fast, the day on which we do not have a covenant. What kind of mystic would have the heart to revel in warmth and light at such a time? As the Mysticat reluctantly acknowledges, he cannot bask with a clear conscience.

After Tisha B'Av, of course, hope steals back in. We read the *Shiv'a D'Nechemta,* the seven Haftarot of prophetic consolation, for the seven weeks leading up to the Days of Awe. But a huge chunk of the sunny summer is paradoxically shadowed by nightmare memories of darkness and violence, of times in which the righteous cry out to a God who has hidden the divine Face. Even an acosmic mystic like the Mysticat is not immune to the outrage of suffering, before which all theologies must ultimately fall silent and in whose presence the only honest prayer is lament.

That is why the light of Tammuz tears at the Mysticat's heart, filling him alternately with ecstasy, yearning, and bitter regret. In the light of Tammuz, the Mysticat becomes an oxymoron: he is precisely a vulnerable, sensuous body of flesh and blood that receives and responds to this light, yet the Mysticat hungers to transcend both the fragility and the dark history of flesh and blood to become a body made of light, at one with the Light of Lights.

30

Picky Picky

TAMMUZ

THE HOLY MYSTICAT IS SOMEWHAT of an ascetic. He eats mostly so that he can do his holy work rather than for sensual pleasure. The staple of his diet is dry cat food. Unlike dogs, who have adventurous palates for people food, the Mysticat rarely partakes of human cuisine. He does have a favorite hors d'oeuvre: small cubes of roast turkey breast. Last week, however, kosher turkey breast was unavailable. I bought some skinned boned chicken thighs to cook, figuring that I'd have some to eat with a green salad, and the Mysticat would have some for his hors d'oeuvre. But when I placed two small cubes before the Mysticat, he looked at them—and at me—with the revulsion of a Maccabean martyr before whom Antiochus IV had placed a chunk of fresh pork. With dignity he rose and stalked away from the offensive morsels. I wanted to offer him something out of the ordinary, and, having read that a healthy treat for a cat was a spoonful of plain yogurt, I placed one attractively on a small plate and set it down before him. He stared at it incredulously for a moment, backing away cautiously in case the blob attacked. Is this true asceticism or just gustatory conservatism, which I tend to attribute to lack of imagination? But isn't that unfairly judgmental on my part?

Currently we are in the midst of the *drei vokhen*—the three weeks that precede the Black Fast of Tisha B'Av, the Ninth of Av, that is the low point of the Jewish year. During this time it is customary not to celebrate or eat luxurious food except on Shabbat. With the arrival of the month of Av, the mourning intensifies. We are mourning not merely the destruction of the Temple but the shattering of the entire *nomos*, the universe of meaning, at whose center that Temple lived. What we mourn is the final destruction of biblical Judaism, which we so painfully replaced with the controversies and complexities of rabbinic Judaism. Instead of prophecy and its certainty, there now exists, as the rabbis put it, an iron curtain between heaven and earth. We must puzzle out what God wants of us, risking terrible mistakes.

When we mourn, we mourn with our whole bodies and our palates too. So in many Jewish communities, tradition tells us to refrain from eating meat from the beginning of Av until the fast on the terrible Ninth, the day on which we have no covenant and God's face is hidden from us. But Rosh Chodesh Av is more than a week away, so I had to dismiss a tentative hypothesis that the Mysticat had rejected the chicken thighs because he had already begun abstaining from meat delicacies. Of necessity, the Mysticat in his current (feline) incarnation continues to eat cat food, since, as he has explained emphatically, he is *not* an herbivore. During the Nine Days themselves, he certainly would not indulge in a meat delicacy. Even I, a simple Jew with no head for mysticism, abstain from meat during this period. By next Monday, cat food will be the only meat in the Adler kitchen. But then how to explain the Mysticat's rejection of both chicken thighs and yogurt? No, I concluded, I had not failed to grasp some ritual or symbolic reason. Possibly the Mysticat was just being picky. Granted, the Mysticat's vagaries concerning sensuous appetite are nothing compared with mine. I give you three guesses which of us is counting calories. But seeing him so disgusted by what looks like perfectly good food to me is an odd sight.

I have lived with the Mysticat for some years, yet at times like these I realize once again that no one can really understand an Other. All we get are occasional flashes of insight and empathy. Love and goodwill must bridge the abyss of our incomprehension. It is said that Jerusalem's destruction was caused by baseless hatred, *sinat chinam,* a plague that still haunts the contemporary world. In preparation for the fast, I am trying to cleanse myself of intolerance for all that is foreign to me, all that I simply do not understand. I can start in my own household. The Mysticat's right to desires and distastes unlike my own must be respected, even when they are mysteries to me.

31

The Mysticat's Churban Bayyit

IN ALIGNMENT WITH THE *CHURBAN BAYYIT*, the destruction of the ancient Temple in Jerusalem, the Holy Mysticat's personal sacred precincts have suffered extensive damage. Water from the condominium apartment above mine leaked into the wall and ceiling dividing our kitchen and dining area from the living room, trickling under the hardwood floor and warping it.

Rooms where the Mysticat, I, and our guests learned Torah and celebrated Shabbat and Yom Tov are reduced to *tohu va-vohu*, the primeval chaos, except that instead of being empty and silent, our chaos is deafeningly noisy. Huge roaring machines dry out sodden walls, now torn open. The ruined hardwood floor is pried up. At first the Mysticat had relocated to the bedroom where he huddled in the closet fasting and lamenting, his sensitive hearing assaulted by the racket. When I pushed the hanging garments aside to offer words of comfort, he stared blindly past me into an indescribable vision of destruction.

After three horrible days, we moved to a short-term residence with the help of Rabbi Courtney Berman, her husband Jeffrey, and Rabbi Benj Fried. The Mysticat, already traumatized, first fought incarceration in the cat carrier. Then upon arrival, he refused to leave it for a full three hours. Although Courtney and I quickly set up the covered litter box that the tzaddik's modesty demands, scratching board, grooming arch, water fountain, and low blue platform with its tempting blue and white dishes of food, he would have none of it. He is in exile, and the salvaged remnants of his world do not assuage his grief. The green tennis ball he would swipe with a powerful paw (only to indulge my enthusiasm for such games) stands in mute testimony to lost moments of levity.

I am reminded that we mourn the *churban bayyit* not because of the destruction of just a building but of a *nomos*, a universe of meaning, an ordered world whose ways were pleasantness and paths were peace (Prov. 3:18). The shattering of a *nomos* is always violent, even when the act is not accompanied by literal bloodshed. When the newly bereaved Reb Mimi Feigelson came to visit us so we could console one another, the Mysticat emerged briefly for the mitzvah of comforting the mourner. When she left, I turned around and the Mysticat was gone. I ransacked the rooms calling his name. There was no sign of him. I have written before about the Mysticat's *bittul ha-yesh* exercises in which the mystic focuses on abnegating his somethingness. It appeared that this time he had been more spectacularly successful than ever before. Could he have absented himself when I opened the door and Reb Mimi and I gazed into each other's faces before she departed? I roamed

the halls in vain. Finally the housekeeping staff located him wedged into an impossibly small space behind the bed. He could not be reached for extrication, but his green eyes were glimpsed burning in the dimness.

Four hours later, the Mysticat resurfaced. Apparently in the interim he had compelled himself to accept exile as a melancholy but irrefutable fact. His is an acceptance without hope. For me to talk to him of rebuilding and return was of no use. All he can do is remember with anguish his lost habitats: the big chair in the study, the piles of holy books on which he loved to recline, the sunlit floor-to-ceiling windows of the living room, all proscribed and rendered hideous in their devastation. I try to hold the hope for him. I sing to him from the fourteen Shirei Ha-Ma'alot, Psalms 120–134, which many scholars believe were songs sung by pilgrims ascending to the Temple. Half of them, like Psalm 126 with which we open the Shabbat Grace after Meals (Birkat Ha-Mazon), are songs of joyous restoration. Others are supplications, but still filled with hope and trust.

As I write, the Mysticat has come to this new and alien window to utter his own supplication in the vernacular—not Yiddish but Cat—lifting his eyes to the hills. The yowls with which he began are followed by unusual sounds he never makes in ordinary conversation. They end in a series of melodic trills. Quietly, his full heart somewhat relieved, the Mysticat lies on the pillow beside me. Somehow we will get through this devastation and displacement, as the lowest point of the year, the Black Fast of Tisha B'Av, approaches.

32

The Mysticat in Exile

AV

TODAY RABBI ZACH ZYSMAN, WHO was in his final year of rabbinical school at Hebrew Union College-Jewish Institute of Religion, came to our temporary residence to work on his final project. He is studying Eikha, the biblical book of Lamentations. As he began to chant the sad, beautiful melody, the Mysticat crept out of the secret hiding place where he had been spending most of his time. Even after Zach finished chanting the chapter, the Mysticat stayed to listen as we argued over translations, Hebrew roots, and grammar and pored over the massive *Brown-Driver-Briggs Hebrew and English Lexicon* I had carried into exile with us. The Bible scholar Kathleen O'Connor writes that for people who have experienced devastation, Eikha is a profoundly comforting book, not because it offers many words of comfort but because it mirrors back to us exactly how horrible devastation is. It permits us to be sad, angry, anguished, and accusatory as we talk to God. It does not try to make us feel something different from what we are genuinely feeling.

The Mysticat sat with us for several hours as the room filled with Torah—painful and difficult Torah, but Torah nonetheless.

When Zach left, both the Mysticat and I felt like Israelites who had just heard that the prophet Ezekiel had a divine vision on the banks of the Chebar Canal in Babylonia: "So God and God's word can find us here too? In that case even exile is bearable!" For the rest of the day the Mysticat sat out in plain sight doing his prayers and meditations. He even had a bite to eat and a few sips of water. As it says in Psalm 119:50, "This is my comfort in my anguish: that Your word gives me life—*Zot nechamati b'oni, ki imratkha chiatni.*" Amen.

33

Flunking Exile

AV

YOU WOULD THINK THAT A Kabbalist would be good at exile. After all, it seems to me that for Lurianic Kabbalah, exile is the ultimate explanation of what is wrong with the universe. Everything is broken. Even Godself is broken, and the pieces are exiled from one another. So I would have thought the Holy Mysticat would immediately mobilize himself and say, "Oh, of course! A shattered world is my natural habitat. I know exactly how to do this. Let me show you!" Instead, the Mysticat is barely eating and drinking. He retreats into hiding at any alarm. At night he sleeps fitfully, his feverish furry body jammed against mine. He does not even bother patrolling for mazikin. "Let the demons have whatever they want" seems to be his attitude. So I'm surprised.

As for me, hey, I'm just the Mysticat's thickheaded gabba'it. I hang out at the shallow end of the pool. A good davening and a satisfying piece of Gemara are about as deep in as I can get. So I couldn't really expect that I would possess the spiritual resources to adapt in any exemplary fashion. In my few lucid moments, however, I am ashamed of my own whining. I miss

my study, my desk, and, oy, my books—my books that have been packed up and put into storage while workers diligently rip out our once shining hardwood floors. I tell myself, "These are just things. You haven't, God forbid, lost a person. Even the stuff you were writing is still intact, for whatever that's worth." But it doesn't sink in very well. It appears to me that the Mysticat and I are both flunking galut.

The sixties folksinger Phil Ochs used to say, "Liberals are ten degrees to the left of center in good times, ten degrees to the right of center if it affects them personally" ("Love Me, I'm a Liberal," *Phil Ochs in Concert*, Elektra Records, 1966). Analogously, now that galut isn't just a theological concept but a pain that's stinging us personally, neither the Mysticat nor I have risen to the occasion very impressively.

I'm fairly certain that the Holy Mysticat is supposed to emerge from his cave to begin actively reconstituting a meaningful universe and embarking on *tikkun*, the repair of what was broken. But I'm afraid to tell him so. In his present mood, he would undoubtedly bite me. Maybe I ought to do more research before raising the issue.

As for me, I'd better settle the practical problems as expeditiously as possible without allowing them to eat up my precious writing time. The first lesson of galut is that it doesn't mean one is now exempt from obligations. All the obligations survive intact. Right now that is a grim fact. However, very dimly, even an oaf like me can sense that it will become a reason to rejoice.

34

The Mysticat's Error

LATE LAST NIGHT, IN THE hyperalert state demanded by his nightly watchcat duties, the Mysticat mistook me for a mazik and bit me twice. True, my bathroom visit had been unscheduled, but how he could have made such an error is still difficult to imagine. As everyone knows, mazikin have feet like chickens and are only two-dimensional (*Berakhot* 3a–b, 6a), whereas I have recognizably human feet—high arched and size 7½—and am solidly three-dimensional. Perhaps my proximity to the bathroom caused the error, since mazikin do lurk around those facilities (*Berakhot* 62a).

The Mysticat was really both impulsive and absent-minded when he used his teeth rather than one of his powerful incantations because mazikin can be quite dangerous. They are implicated in building collapse, rot, decay, and various sorts of harm to human beings (*Berakhot* 3b, 43b; *Sanhedrin* 101a). Moreover, if he had just used the proper incantation, I would not have been affected since I am *not* a mazik. I was as offended at being mistaken for a mazik as my sister once was when a complete stranger mistook her for the egregious Linda Tripp.

Consequently, the atmosphere was rather frigid as I prepared the Mysticat's morning repast, and I slammed his bowl down without the usual cordial greetings. The Mysticat's appetite was unimpaired by these subtle signs of displeasure. There does seem to be a high correlation between maleness and obliviousness to an atmosphere. He ate, *bensched*, and betook himself to his usual meditations and prayers without comment. But later that day, having realized that I was harboring resentment, he presented himself in the bedroom, where I was having a Shabbat nap, as the lovely Shabbat melody "Mah Yedidut" puts it, "Sleep is praiseworthy / it restores the soul—*Ha-sheinah meshubachat / ke-dat nefesh meshivat.*"

In one powerful leap, the Mysticat was on the bed. He settled himself full length on top of me with his face an inch from mine. With the courtesy of a scholarly feline who knows that his Person has thought seriously about *I and Thou*, he gazed deeply into my eyes, just like the cat with whom Martin Buber recounts such a moment in *I and Thou*. Then he briefly touched his nose to mine. I could be only moved at this acknowledgment of me and the theology of relationship I espouse, especially since the Mysticat, a committed acosmicist, believes that "I" and "thou" are illusory boundaries because we are all part of God. I am still unclear about how this translates into an ethics, but whatever his reasoning, the Mysticat concluded that he had injured me and needed to make amends. Now that Tisha B'Av is past, we had better all be setting our thoughts and actions toward *teshuvah*. I only hope I will do as well as he.

35

The Mysticat Comes Home

ELUL/TISHREI

TOWARD THE END OF ELUL, the Holy Mysticat, *shlita*, arrived back home. He was astonished to be there, having despaired of ever seeing home again. Home was dusty, dirty, and crowded with stacked cartons of books, pots, and china. The premises swarmed with electricians, plumbers, painters, and repair people, but blessed light poured from the great windows, and the Mysticat gratefully surrendered himself to contemplation and praise. The task of transforming domestic chaos into serenely ordered cosmos could be safely delegated to his gabba'it.

By Erev Yom Kippur, everything that mattered (to the Mysticat, that is) was unpacked, immaculate, and in its proper place. The only room not yet organized was the study. The holy books stood ready in the bookcases, to the Mysticat's satisfaction, but files were still stacked haphazardly on the big desk. Technicians came and went for weeks, vainly trying to ascertain why the laptop had no internet access and was no longer on speaking terms with the wireless printer. Hopefully this conundrum will be resolved before Kol Nidre.

At the center of all this activity, I find myself conflicted about my duties and priorities. On the one hand, I share the Mysticat's eagerness for shining order to be restored so we can properly honor these Days of Awe. On the other hand, I am impatient to resume the interrupted work on my book, which the Mysticat finds baffling and even annoying. He heartily concurs with Ecclesiastes (Kohelet), whose book we will chant on Shabbat Chol Ha-moed Sukkot: "The making of books is without limit and much study is a wearying of the flesh" (Eccles. 12:12). Like most teachers of esoterica, the Mysticat is convinced that knowledge should be given orally, master to student, and this wisdom communicated in a few cryptic meows, so much the better. As Abraham Ibn Ezra so famously said, "Those who understand, will understand—*Ha-meyvin yavin*" (Ibn Ezra on Gen. 12:6). Moreover, according to the Mysticat, if a gabba'it does write, surely her proper subject matter is the wisdom and miracles of the tzaddik as she has witnessed them, not her own pitiful attempts at theology.

I told the tzaddik that, frankly, the standards of seemly behavior for a gabba'it were of no interest to me. Moreover, the fact that our theologies differ is not news to the Mysticat. The Mysticat is a Kabbalist and acosmicist. I am in love with Otherness, with building rickety bridges between I and thou and between I and Thou. I am not very good at making theology—no human is—but I have to try.

Fortunately before the atmosphere deteriorated further, the Mysticat and I recollected what the Days of Awe are actually for and retracted our claws, the Mysticat literally and I metaphorically. We do love each other. We don't want to be hurtful. We do want to give our best efforts to the task at hand: preparing our souls for the Sabbath of Sabbaths that begins this evening, a day of holy joy that feeds our souls, while we temporarily free ourselves from the demands of our bodies. Then, too, the Mysticat and I will acknowledge that no creature of flesh and blood really knows the unknowable One for whom (or which) we hunger and thirst, like creatures in a parched land without water (Ps. 63:2). We can only piece together our tattered truths with one another's help. May loving-kindness, mutual respect, and peace infuse our life and work in the year ahead. To all, *g'mar chatimah tovah*. May you be sealed in the Book of Life for a year of fruitfulness and peace.

36

Eyes Closed, Soul Wide Open

———

2018

I REMEMBER THE HOLY MYSTICAT saying his Bedtime
Shema on my bed, his eyes tightly shut. I, too, shut my eyes
when I say Shema and cover them with my hand, a gesture
the Talmud attributes to the great Rabbi Yehudah Ha-Nasi
(*Berakhot* 13b). Shema's opening imperative is "Hear!" and
not "See!" That, I was taught, is why we cover our eyes. Of
course, *shema* does not only mean "hear" in the literal sense.
The majority rabbinic opinion (*Berakhot* 13a) that the Shema
may be said in any language rests on the assumption that the
word means not only "hear" but "understand." My ears may
take in a torrent of sounds in a language I do not speak, but if
I cannot separate the torrent into intelligible words, all I hear
is noise. But hearing the words and comprehending them is
only the beginning of understanding. More profound understandings happen deep inside us. Ancient writers located the
site of understanding in the liver or the heart. Sometimes they
saw it as a whole-body experience. Psalm 35:10 exclaims, "All
my bones are saying, God, who is like you?—*Kol atzmotai
tomarna, Adonai mi-kamokha*." The beautiful Shabbat and

holiday prayer Nishmat quotes this verse. The Mysticat had this whole-body experience as naturally as breathing. For me it is rare. But all serious daveners know that to go deeper inside ourselves, closing our eyes helps.

I have memorized chunks of most of my Amidah so that I need not open my eyes to read. The Mysticat prayed entirely by memory and had internalized incalculable amounts of Talmud and Zohar to boot, but of course, the Mysticat had an unfair advantage: he could absorb the content of books by lying on top of them. Yet the question that no one has ever answered for me is, What is supposed to happen inside us when we plumb our depths? When I asked the Mysticat, he bit me—a mere admonitory nip—but this hint that the Mysticat's spiritual process was none of my business disinclined me to pursue the matter.

One of my first Talmud teachers explained that the assumption in chapter 5 of *Tractate Berakhot* is that to pray the Amidah, we enter a mild trance state. We are meant to remain just aware enough of our surroundings to shorten our prayer if a scorpion or the local sociopath is heading one's way. This information was helpful but insufficient. Altered states of consciousness are hard to describe. Most memorabilia from 1960s psychedelic trips are incoherent or boring—and sometimes both. My one hands-on psychedelic experiment was unenlightening. An imposing rebbe appeared to me in a vision addressing me by my Hebrew name and demanded that I never take the stuff again.

Chemicals were no help. The Mysticat's teeth discouraged further interrogation. So I altered my hypothesis. Maybe our alterations of consciousness are as individualized as fingerprints or DNA. Maybe I did not need to discover what the Mysticat's Amidah was like. Discovering what mine could be was enough and that could be accomplished by withdrawing under my big tallit, closing my eyes, and descending into the deep silence within myself. Other daveners can do this more quickly. In minyan, I finish the silent Amidah barely in time for communal repetition and the Kedushah prayer. Sometimes during my silence, whispered words bloom into multiple resonances. Connections to Torah, Psalms, or even secular poetry flash by. Music hovers at the edges of words. Teachings replay, sometimes in the voices of teachers.

When I try to imagine the depths of the Mysticat's prayer, I imagine it as more tactile and visual, less wordy, and more brilliant than mine. Perhaps behind his eyelids, fireworks of arcane images formed and dissolved in colored light. Perhaps he saw the light of the Garden of Eden, one of the metaphors for the perfect, untainted place to which we return when our lives are done. Perhaps, perhaps.

Last year, the Mysticat peacefully closed his eyes forever. Perhaps in the darkness he has reunited with the limitless God he sought so passionately to repair. The seventeenth-century Christian poet Henry Vaughan gives me an image the Mysticat might have liked: "There is in God . . . / a deep but dazzling darkness. . . . / O for that night where I in Him / Might live invisible and dim!" May his memory illuminate and be a blessing.

Appendix A:
The Cycle of the Jewish Year

FROM TISHREI TO ELUL, THE Jewish calendar has a rhythm all its own, one that charts our spiritual and religious lives. The dates on the secular calendar stretch from midnight to midnight, but Jewish days begin at sunset and last until the next sunset. Since ancient times, the Jewish months have followed the course of the moon (with adjustments to the solar seasons). The moon, which waxes, wanes, disappears, then reappears—beginning the cycle again—

Tishrei	(September–October)
Cheshvan	(October–November)
Kislev	(November–December)
Tevet	(December–January)
Shevat	(January–February)
Adar	(February–March)
Nisan	(March–April)
Iyyar	(April–May)
Sivan	(May–June)
Tammuz	(June–July)
Av	(July–August)
Elul	(August–September)

represents the rhythms of our spiritual and physical lives. Just as the moon grows, diminishes, and is renewed, so has the fate of the People Israel throughout the many cycles of our long history.

The Days of Awe

Our Jewish calendar counts from Tishrei to Tishrei just as the secular calendar counts from January 1 to January 1. The holy day of Rosh HaShanah occurs on the first and second days of the month of Tishrei (September–October) and is the spiritual opening of the new year. Yet unlike the raucous, giddy celebration of the secular New Year, the mood of Rosh HaShanah is deeply introspective. Moreover, rather than being a stand-alone celebration, Rosh HaShanah opens a festival season, a ten-day period—the Days of Awe—that culminates in the fast of Yom Kippur, the Day of Atonement on the tenth of Tishrei. These days are also called "the Ten Days of Teshuvah."

Teshuvah, often translated as "repentance," really means "returning" or "turning around." This act is not a single one but a process of becoming accountable: we evaluate our actions, repent for the bad choices, apologize to those we have offended, and make amends for injuries. Because God cannot forgive us for what we have done to another human being, we must deal directly with the persons we have injured. We should be able to show progress by Yom Kippur; although, Maimonides, the tenth-century scholar, says we can be certain that our *teshuvah* is complete only when we encounter a similar situation and make a better choice. *Teshuvah* is not a once-a-year event, however. All year long, a confessional prayer is included in the weekday Amidah, but some of us need a deadline to get us moving. These ten days offer a last opportunity before accounts on the past year are closed.

Yom Kippur, which involves twenty-five hours of prayer and fasting, is like the repairing of a relationship—in this case, the relationship between the estranged lovers God and the People Israel. Much is demanded of us when we repair a relationship, but returning to one another is healing and joyous. Fasting is not the point of Yom Kippur but rather a tool for focusing on what matters most. The activities from which we refrain on Yom Kippur—eating, drinking, and sexual activity—remind us of our physicality and that we are time-limited, temporary creatures. The relationships we take for granted could be suddenly ended.

Many other cultures also use fasting, both as a way of focusing and as a tool for altering consciousness. That is why many Native American cultures use it in vision quests. If you persist until the final service of Yom Kippur, Ne'ilah, you and your community are likely to experience a euphoria that intensifies your sense of having been purified and given another chance at being a better Jew.

During the multiple services of Yom Kippur, we recite confessions both silently as individuals and aloud as the corporate entity of the People Israel. We do so because "All Israel are guarantors for one another" (*Shevuot* 39a). When we confess aloud, we assume communal responsibility for one another's actions. For example, if someone stole and we did not intervene, or if we did not offer destitute people an option other than theft, the whole community shares this guilt.

The Three Pilgrimage Festivals

On the three pilgrimage festivals—Sukkot, Pesach/Passover, and Shavuot/Feast of Weeks—pilgrims traveled to Jerusalem to offer sacrifices (see Num. 28 and 29 and Deut. 16:1–17).

Sukkot

Within the week after Yom Kippur concludes, the festival of Sukkot begins on the fifteen of Tishrei (September–October). Sukkot ("Huts") is a harvest festival celebrating the gathering of the crops. A sukkah is a temporary shelter in the fields roofed with leafy branches or wood. This shelter shades harvesters from noon heat and provides a resting place as they gather or guard crops. The stories say that our ancestors lived in huts while wandering the wilderness for forty years before entering the Promised Land. Even today, those who can will build a sukkah in their yard and eat their meals there. The festival of Sukkot, which lasts a week, begins right before the rainy season in Israel, so a major theme is hope for the blessing of rain, without which nothing can survive. Sukkot is called "the time of our joy" (*z'man simchatenu*). The harvest ensures feasting and plenty. Singing, dancing, and processionals characterize Sukkot services, along with the ritual waving of the two special Sukkot symbols: the lulav, a palm branch with willows and myrtle attached to it, and the etrog, a citron, first mentioned in Leviticus 23:40. Sukkot's themes of joy and abundance are balanced by a sobering awareness that they (and we) are temporary. Hence, on Shabbat Sukkot, we chant the book of Kohelet (Ecclesiastes), which is about balancing vulnerability and joy.

The last day(s) of Sukkot have the status of a new holiday: Shemini Atzeret, the Eighth Day. On it, we begin to mention God's blessing of rain to the third blessing of the Amidah. Outside Israel, Conservative and Orthodox Jews celebrate a ninth day, Simchat Torah, or the Celebration of the Torah. Amid singing, dancing, and processionals (*hakafot*), we rejoice with the Torah. We finish chanting the Torah portion that concludes Deuteronomy and immediately begin again with Genesis. In Israel and in Reform communities around the world, Simchat Torah is conflated with Shemini Atzeret and observed on the eighth day.

Pesach

The second of the pilgrimage festivals is Pesach, or Passover. Lasting a week, it celebrates our liberation from Egyptian slavery. Pesach begins on the fifteenth of Nisan (March–April), the month of spring. In Temple times, pilgrims journeyed to Jerusalem to partake of the paschal lamb sacrifice in family groups. The telling of the Pesach story, the Haggadah, originated as part of this festive meal. After the Temple's destruction, the rabbis transformed the Haggadah, or Telling, into the seder. The entire meal became the frame for the Haggadah. After the Temple was destroyed, the rabbis compared the household table with the Temple altar (*Chagigah* 27a). The table is the sacred place of the household. Blessings are made there. Torah is studied there. The poor are invited in and nourished. Hence, the table is the logical place for reciting and discussing the Haggadah.

Pesach has food restrictions. Leavened foods (such as bread, alcohol, baking powder, and grain vinegar) may not be eaten. Strict observance requires eradicating even crumbs or dribbles of them in a rigorous housecleaning before the holiday and special kitchenware is brought out. Instead of bread, we eat matzah, the cheap, fuel-efficient flatbread of slavery, which also turns out to be the ideal journey bread for wanderers in the wilderness.

As an agricultural festival, Pesach occurs at a time after both the fall and winter rains. The crops need dew to finish growing. Hence, at Pesach, Sephardic and Arabic Jewish liturgies switch from praising God for bringing rain to praising God for dew. All liturgies—Ashkenazic, Sephardic, and other ones—include a piyyut (prayer-poem) asking for abundant dew and drop the liturgical mention of rain in the third blessing of the Amidah. The book we chant on the intermediate Shabbat of Pesach is Shir HaShirim, or Song of Songs, to celebrate love and relationships, especially the relationship between Israel and God. Although our first patriarchs and matriarchs had histories with God, we as a people first encountered God during the oppressions of and liberation from slavery.

The Omer and Shavuot

The Omer, a barley sacrifice, was offered in the Temple from the second day of Pesach for seven weeks until the third pilgrimage festival, Shavuot. That was harvesttime for the barley crop. The custom of counting the day and week of the Omer aloud every night creates an organic link between Pesach and Shavuot, which occurs fifty days later on the sixth of Sivan (May–June). Counting the Omer links the freedom from slavery we gained at Pesach with the covenantal responsibility we assumed when we received the Torah on Shavuot. Responsibility is the privilege of the free. Slaves are not even permitted responsibility for their children. An owner can sell children or sell parents away from children. Freedom makes responsibility possible, but people must commit themselves to shouldering responsibility. Without responsibility, freedom devolves into impulse and egotism. Learning the Torah's unfolding revelation teaches us how to use freedom to be responsible to and for our relationship partners, human and Divine. On the first day of Shavuot, we stand and reconfirm our responsibility for the Sinai Covenant as we read the story of the giving and acceptance of the Torah in Exodus 19–20. But the special book we chant is the book of Ruth, which relates the acceptance of the Torah by the first non-Israelite to commit herself to the People Israel and the God of Israel: Ruth, the ancestress of King David. The story is set in premonarchal Israel at the time of the spring harvests. Naomi, who fled Israel during a famine with her husband and sons, returns a childless widow. She had intended to return alone, but her Moabite daughter-in-law Ruth refuses to leave her. "Your people shall be my people and your God my God," she vows (Ruth 1:16). The lesson of the book of Ruth is that Torah requires not merely legal observance but generous loving-kindness (*chesed*). *Chesed* moves us to be responsible creatively. The chain of kindnesses that Ruth and other characters join restores life and hope to the whole society and points toward the redemption of the world.

Other Holy Days

Chanukah

The festival of Chanukah, observed for eight nights and days starting on the twenty-fifth of Kislev (November–December), commemorates the rededication of the Second Temple at the time of the Maccabean Revolt against the Seleucid Empire. The history behind the holiday is complicated. After the death of Alexander the Great, his empire was divided up among rival warlords. Judea belonged first to the Egyptian Ptolemies and then was handed over to the Seleucid Empire. At first, like Alexander and the Ptolemies, the Seleucids did not meddle with the religion of their subjects. But Antiochus IV intervened to support Hellenizing Jews in their civil war with traditionalists. He invaded Jerusalem, despoiled the Temple, and prohibited the practice of Judaism. The Maccabees, led by a traditionalist priestly family, won and purified the Temple. The aftermath is less pretty. The Maccabean leaders made themselves kings and became violent and corrupt, reaching their nadir at the time proto-rabbinic Judaism was developing.

The rabbis despised the Maccabean kings. They refused to canonize the book of Maccabees, which, consequently, appears in Catholic, Eastern Orthodox, and some Protestant Bibles but not in the Tanakh, the Hebrew Bible. Yet Chanukah was already an entrenched holiday. So the festival was reframed around the story of a miracle that occurred during the purification of the Temple, in which one day's oil supply burned for eight days.

The miracle, then, is about light and spirit. The rabbis do not exalt militarism or martyrdom, as the book of Maccabees does. Chanukah occurs right around the winter solstice at the darkest time of the year. The imagery about light and hope returning is poignant. The only legal requirement for Chanukah observance is to light the eight-branched Chanukah menorah, a miniature version of the great menorah (which had seven). Traditional treats include latkes, potato pancakes, for Ashkenazic Jews, and *sufganiot*, jelly doughnuts, for Sephardic and Israeli Jews.

Tu B'Shevat: The New Year of the Trees

The Mishnah (*Rosh HaShanah* 1:1) names not one but four New Years, all occurring during different months. It names Tu B'Shevat, the fifteenth of the month of Shevat (January–February), as the New Year of the Trees. In ancient times, this day was a deadline for determining tithing obligations to the Temple but now is celebrated as a time for honoring trees and their fruit. This holy day has no required observances, but some people hold a Tu B'Shevat Seder, a small version of a Pesach Seder at which they study texts about trees and eat fruit.

Trees are powerful symbols in Judaism. Think of the Tree of the Knowledge of Good and Evil and the Tree of Life in Genesis 2. The Menorah of the Tabernacle (Exod. 37:17–24) and, later, the Jerusalem Temple, as well as our little Chanukah menorot, are stylized representations not just of a tree but a tree on fire that is not consumed. Moses hears God speaking out of such a tree in Exodus 3. A tree on fire that is not consumed is an anomaly and a riddle, much like the Jewish People. Trees are deeply rooted, sturdy, and long lived. Tanakh, and especially the book of Psalms, is full of them. A central symbol in Jewish mysticism is the upside-down Tree of the Sefirot, whose roots are in heaven and whose branches descend through all the worlds of being.

The Festival of Purim

Purim, celebrated on the fourteenth of Adar (February–March) and in walled cities on the fifteenth of Adar, celebrates our narrow escape from annihilation by an ethnic group whose leader, Haman, rose to power within the Persian Empire. The story of

Purim is told in the book of Esther, the only festival book that must be chanted from a hand-scribed scroll (Megillah). The Megillah reading is lengthy but rowdy. Booing and noisemaker-wielding participants drown out every mention of the villain.

The book of Esther is fictional rather than historical. Even the villainous ethnic group, the Amalekites, are legendary. But the threat of annihilation is very real in Jewish history, as you will see if you skim the "Timeline of the Jewish World." One response to that looming threat is Purim, this carnival of a holy day, full of eating, drinking, joking, masquerading, playing games, and sharing satirical commentary.

One Purim obligation is to send gifts of food to one another. In Ashkenazic communities, the distinctive Purim treats are hamantaschen ("Haman pockets"), which are pastries stuffed with sweet fillings. In Sephardic and Arabic Jewish communities, the treat is *oznei Haman* ("Haman's ears"), fried pastries drizzled with honey. Because we never celebrate without giving to those in need, another obligation is gifts of money to the poor. A distinctive feature of Purim is satirical plays, Purim *shpiels*, performed in synagogues and rabbinical seminaries. On Purim, nothing is too holy to be laughed at: rabbis, scholars, institutional policies, and politics, both local and national.

You have to believe that sacredness exists to have permission to laugh at it. A famous Chasidic pun is *Yom Kippurim yom k'Purim*—Yom Kippur is a day like Purim. Perhaps this means that if you are doing it correctly—fasting and feasting—solemnity and laughter should take you to the same holy place. The Holy Mysticat was never enthusiastic about Purim, but, with all due respect, his sense of humor was minimal.

Lag B'Omer

Lag B'Omer falls on the thirty-third day of the seven-week period between Passover and Shavuot (during Iyyar: April–May), during which the Israelites would bring sheaves of their barley harvest (*omer* means "sheath") to the Temple as a gratitude offering. The Hebrew letters *lamed* and *gimel*, which make up the acronym "Lag," have the combined numerical value of thirty-three. While Lag B'Omer is a minor holiday, it is a festive one, during which Jews, particularly in Israel, celebrate with picnics, bonfires, and weddings.

Tisha B'Av: The Ninth of Av

The Ninth of Av is in a class by itself. This solemn day of lament and fasting commemorates the destruction of the First Temple (in 586 BCE) and the Second Temple (70 CE). While other fasts occur throughout the Jewish year, this is one of the most significant fasts. During the course of Jewish history, Tisha B'Av became a sponge for all the catastrophes suffered by the Jewish people. On it, we mourn the destruction of both Temples, the expulsions of Jews from their land, the massacres of the Crusades, the Holocaust (Shoah), and contemporary violence against Jewish communities.

During the three weeks that lead up to the Ninth of Av (July–August), some communities abstain from certain pleasures, such as concerts, haircuts, or parties. A common custom is to not eat meat from the beginning of Av until after the fast, except for Shabbat.

Even Shabbat is darkened by the countdown. On the three Shabbatot preceding Tisha B'Av, the Haftarot, or prophetic readings that accompany the Torah reading, admonish the people for injustices and oppressions that anger God. These readings are called the Three of Admonition (in Aramaic, the Tlata D' Puranuta). The last of the three, before Tisha B'Av, is chanted in the chilling melody of the book of Lamentations (Eikha) rather than in the usual chant for the prophetic portion.

Observance of Tisha B'Av has all the stringencies associated with Yom Kippur. But in contrast to Yom Kippur's hopefulness and solemn joy, the Ninth of Av is a scream of despair that dramatically enacts a descent into deceit and destruction. On this day the synagogue sanctuary, the heart of Jewish order and meaning, is thrown into disorder. In some synagogues, the Holy Ark (Aron Ha-Kodesh), where the Torah scrolls rest, is either draped in black or shrouded in a white sheet, like a corpse. Some overturn the chairs on the bima, or altar. During the services held in this chaotic environment, congregants sit on the floor and chant the book of Lamentations in the saddest of all Jewish melodies. We sing special poems of lament called Kinot. It is customary on Tisha B'Av not to greet or acknowledge our friends. We file silently out of services in the evening and the next morning. As a sign of this terrible despair and estrangement from God, we do not wear tefillin at the Shacharit, or morning service, as we usually do on weekdays. Instead we don them at an early Mincha, or afternoon service, held just after half the daylight hours are over.

From Mincha on, hope increases. The Talmud (Yerushalmi *Berakhot* 2:4) teaches that the Messiah is born on Tisha B'Av. The hope of redemption is reborn and with it the determination to help bring about that redemption. The Torah portion following the Ninth of Av is always Va-Etchanan, containing the second version of the Ten Commandments (Deut. 5). We follow our Tisha B'Av dive into despair by rising as a community on Shabbat to recontract the covenant.

Then we begin to look forward to the next month, Elul (August–September), so that we may prepare ourselves for the Days of Awe. Liturgically, Tisha B'Av is the necessary prelude to the renewal of the month of Elul and its preparation for the Days of Awe in Tishrei (September–October). The seven Shabbat prophetic readings leading up to the Days of Awe are called the Shiv'a D'Nechemta, the Seven of Consolation. Their themes of hope and restoration accompany us on our return to God so that on Rosh Hashanah we can begin again.

Appendix B:
What Is Kabbalah?

MYSTICISM, IN ALL RELIGIONS OR philosophical traditions, involves the quest for higher spiritual awareness. Mysticism's primary focus is on becoming more intimately connected to God, other Divine beings (angels, saints, demigods, or spirit guides or guardians), Nature itself, or (in rarer cases) demonic beings. Mysticism is often heavily philosophical or theological, contemplative, and inner focused; however, sometimes it may also include practical magic. In all cases, this quest is exceedingly complex, nuanced, and, most often, esoteric.

Kabbalah is the blanket term for Judaism's mystical tradition. The word literally means "That Which Is Received." Kabbalah has evolved generally through several phases, most in the last millennium, and continues to grow and change.

The main schools of thought, key ideas, and texts of Kabbalah are listed below.

Merkavah Mysticism: Turn of the Common Era to Third Century CE

No extant independent texts of Merkavah Mysticism are known, but stories and teachings in Talmud incorporate its elements. Merkavah Mysticism is based chiefly on interpretation of Ezekiel 1 and other appearances of divinities in the Prophets. Adherents of Merkavah Mysticism, who practiced in small circles, such as that of Rabbi Akiva and his students, attempted consciousness-raising trances with accompanying movement. Practitioners of Merkavah Mysticism were known as Yoredei ha-Merkavah ("Those Who Descend to the Chariot").

Heichalot Mysticism: Fourth to Eleventh Century

Heichalot Mysticism is the next evolution of Merkavah Mysticism. Heichalot ("palace" or "sanctuary") Mysticism's chief texts were *Heichalot Rabbati* and *Heichalot Zutarti*, which agglomerated interpretations of Genesis 1 and 2. Its adherents focused on angelology and elaborate midrashim about the various Heavenly dwellings with an eye toward experiencing visions thereof. Those interested in practical magic began including those ideas, as well as neo-Platonic and astrological ideas.

Pre-Zoharic Kabbalah: Eighth to Fourteenth Century

Pre-Zoharic Kabbalah's chief texts are *Sefer Yetzirah* (Book of Formation), whose author is unknown but is attributed to various rabbis, Solomon, Avraham, or Adam; and *Sefer ha-Bahir* (Book of Brilliance), whose author is unknown, possibly redacted by Rabbi Yitzchak Sagi Nehor, and attributed to Rabbi Nechuniyah ben Hakana. This Kabbalah represented a major shift away from anthropomorphic imagery and toward envisioning God as complex, essentially unknowable, and aphysical (God as energy).

Zoharic Kabbalah: Thirteenth Century Onward

The chief texts of Zoharic Kabbalah are the Zohar and *Tikkunei Zohar*, attributed to Rabbi Shimon ben Yochai but almost certainly composed by the mystical circle directed by Rabbi Moshe ben ShemTov de Leon, a Sephardic Kabbalist living in Spain. The Zohar becomes the primary core text of all Kabbalah. It introduces the concept of the layers and transmigration of souls.

Lurianic Kabbalah: Sixteenth Century Onward

Lurianic Kabbalah is named for Rabbi Yitzchak Luria, also called the ARI (for Elahi Rav Yitzchak, "the Godly Rabbi Isaac") or Ha-Ari HaKadosh ("the Sacred Lion"), who took Zoharic Kabbalah and developed a radical new cosmology and theological framework around it. According to Lurianic Kabbalah, God comprises a complicated set of energies, of which we may be a part. Among other ideas, Lurianic Kabbalah envisions Creation as the result of a primal catastrophe within the Divine and understands the purpose of life as "raising up" broken Divine energy to restore God's natural balance of being.

Chasidism: Seventeenth Century Onward

Chasidism is a populist ecstatic movement founded in pre-Enlightenment and early Enlightenment Eastern Europe. It is based heavily in Kabbalah, especially Zoharic and Lurianic Kabbalah. Chasidism shifted the primary focus of Jewish life away from text study and toward joyful observance of the mitzvot as potent mystical acts with cosmic significance.

Jewish Renewal: 1970s Onward

As a movement, Jewish Renewal is a wide spectrum of theologies and observances. Its transdenominational philosophy is grounded in neo-Chasidic teachers like Rabbi Zalman Schachter-Shalomi, Rabbi Shlomo Carlebach, Rabbi Arthur Green, and others and is deeply influenced by Kabbalah.

As more works on and English translations of Kabbalah become available—both from the Orthodox and non-Orthodox worlds—more Kabbalistic concepts begin working their way into a Jewish mainstream that is thirsty for alternative perspectives, theological flexibility, and creative, intensive spiritual practice.

Appendix C:
Jewish Perspectives on Sacred Texts

ONE FACTOR THAT DISTINGUISHES JEWS from many kinds of Christians is our understanding of what constitutes sacred text and how we engage with it. First of all we have the Hebrew Bible, or Tanakh, an acronym for the three categories of biblical books: Torah in the strictest sense of the word (the Five Books of Moses: Genesis, Exodus, Leviticus, Numbers, and Deuteronomy), Nevi'im (Prophets), and Ketuvim (Writings). Jews read scripture in the original Hebrew and in translation, usually side by side. It is worth noting that some of the later books are ordered differently when they appear in the Christian New Testament, which also includes books considered by Jewish tradition to be apocrypha. Tanakh is a heterogenous collection of traditions and documents from about twelfth century BCE to about third century BCE. That is about nine hundred years, slightly longer than the span between the medieval poet Chaucer and Bob Dylan. It should not surprise us that biblical books arise out of different geographical settings and represent multiple perspectives, sometimes contradicting or reinterpreting one another. Interestingly the scholars who assembled the biblical canon between 200 BCE and 200 CE did not try to reconcile the contradictions. They left them all in. It appears that both biblical writers and canonizers believed that truth is complicated and it can embrace contradictions.

The Five Books of Moses are the texts handwritten on a scroll that are chanted aloud in weekly portions in synagogues, followed by a chanted excerpt from the Prophets. On special occasions, books from Ketuvim are also chanted in the synagogue service. Chanting or singing is the most ancient way of telling stories in many cultures. For centuries, Torah was an oral storytelling tradition. In ancient Greece, Homer's epics were chanted, accompanied by a lyre. Singing is a powerful aid to memorization, which is the way we take texts inside us, so that they are always available to us.

Rabbinic Judaism calls the first five books *Torah she'bikh-tav* ("Written Torah"). By extension, the rabbis sometimes refer to the whole Hebrew Bible, Tanakh, as "Written Torah." Rabbinic Judaism adds to the Tanakh the *Torah she'be'al peh* ("Oral Torah"). Thus, the traditions and legal rulings of the Talmudic rabbis, the stories and interpretations of midrash, and even later, codes and commentaries all become part of the sacred canon. The implication is that Torah is not a one-time revelation. Torah unfolds in time as many scholars clarify or contest one another's understandings. As the twentieth-century philosopher Simon Rawidowicz points out, the rabbinic concept of Oral Torah embeds interpretation into revelation itself. Interpretation is not regarded as a secondary process to find out what the text *really* means. Rabbinic interpretation tends to deny that texts have a single correct meaning. Sacred texts are sacred not because they teach just one timeless truth but because they are inexhaustible. We can return to them repeatedly and draw new insights.

The interpretations are Torah, just as the Hebrew Bible is Torah. Instead of one book recording infallible words from the past, concentric rings of sacred texts beget a noisy, living tradition to which every Jew may contribute if he, she, or they have a compelling new insight into the ancient words.

Interpretation is not entirely freewheeling. The text cannot mean anything you would like it to mean. The Talmudic rabbis created a set of interpretive ground rules and later interpreters added others. All agree that a good interpreter has to account for the words in the text and offer a valid interpretation that is plausible to other rational people. But classical scholars generally acknowledge that interpreters can and will differ about interpretations.

That is why Jewish text study is a relational rather than solitary act. The books of Tanakh argue with one another, and Talmud and midrash are conversations among many voices. The first legal codes, the *Mishneh Torah* of Maimonides and the *Shulchan Arukh* of Rabbi Yosef Karo, tried to present a single authoritative voice telling people definitively what to do. In the editions that followed, however, the authors' texts were forced into the center of the page, while columns of commentary crowded the edges, explaining or vociferously disagreeing. All these commentaries and disagreements are now part of the body of sacred text we study today. Reasoned disagreement is part of the process of Torah study and a path to the Holy. Even the Holy Mysticat, who viewed himself as an authoritative scholar, secretly relished his interpretive disagreements with his mouthy assistant (his gabba'it).

It is important to note that both the competence and authority to engage in Torah interpretation were, for a long time, closed to Jews who were not part of a cisgendered masculine elite. Women and LGBTQ people have had to talk their way into the conversation of Jewish tradition. As they now bring their own experiences and conditions into the community of interpreters, new truths are emerging from the inexhaustible texts—the Torah that only these new interpreters can teach.

According to twentieth-century philosopher Emmanuel Levinas, both human others and the Divine Other offer us an opportunity to learn what we could not know independently. That is revelation. For Levinas, it follows that revelation impels action. Truths are not abstract. They are embodied and often painful. What revelation reveals to us is *our obligation to do something*. Just as revelation leads to interpretation, it also leads to responsibility. As we said at Mount Sinai when we received the Torah, "We will do and we will understand—*na'aseh v'nishma*" (Exod. 24:7).

Appendix D:
Anatomy of the Talmud

THE TALMUD IS A COLLECTION, not a single book. Its many tractates were compiled over hundreds of years. Rather than one author's voice, Talmudic tractates consist of many voices. Talmud is like the internet in the way it is structured so that speakers who lived at different times and in different places appear to be in conversation (for more on this see Jonathan Rosen's *The Talmud and the Internet*). The Talmud consists of two layers: Mishnah and Gemara. Mishnah, a terse collection of early rabbinic legal traditions written in Hebrew, was passed down from teacher to students through memorization and recitation by generations of scholars known as the Tannaim. The subject matter of the Mishnah is organized into six orders (sedarim). At the end of this section, you will find a list of the orders of the Mishnah and their topics.

Around 200 CE, Rabbi Yehudah Ha-Nasi, head of the Sanhedrin in the Land of Israel, ordered that the Mishnah be written down. The decision was a prescient one. Over the next few centuries, the political situation deteriorated so badly that scholars fled in every direction. Had the Mishnah not been written down, it would have been lost. Without the Mishnah, there could have been no Gemara.

In about 300 CE, legal traditions that were not included in the Mishnah were collected into a supplementary source called Tosefta, meaning "Supplement." Scholars of the Gemara cite Tosefta in their discussions because it sometimes adds to or clarifies the Mishnah and sometimes contradicts it. Jewish legal scholars thrive on arguments and contradictions.

The Gemara, consisting of lengthy commentaries on the Mishnah, was compiled by scholars known as the amoraim. There are two Gemaras and hence two Talmuds: the Jerusalem Talmud and the Babylonian Talmud. Both are written in Aramaic. The tractates of both Talmuds are grouped according to the six orders of the Mishnah. Mishnah tractates dealing with agricultural law in the Land of Israel and donations to the now-destroyed Temple have no Gemara.

The Jerusalem Talmud, which contains commentaries on the Mishnah by scholars in the Land of Israel, was compiled between approximately 350 and 450. Its process was hurried and incomplete because of the chaos that accompanied the disintegration of the Roman Empire. Moreover, after Christianity became the official religion of the Roman Empire in the fourth century, persecution of Jews in the Land of Israel became severe and most of the Jewish population emigrated.

The Babylonian Talmud, compiled between 300 and 700, contains a much more expansive Gemara. Because Jews had more legal autonomy in Babylonia, these scholars developed an impressive body of case law. Yet Gemara is not organized like a Western law code. Instead, these legal conversations are discursive, associative, and meandering. You might think of Mishnah as the legal equivalent of short-term psychotherapy—you focus on a particular topic, identify the possible responses to it, and hopefully come to a conclusion by the time you're done. Gemara is more like the legal equivalent of long-term psychoanalysis. Major themes emerge over time, and the group explores them broadly, questioning legal definitions, citing cases, speculating on philosophy, telling stories to exemplify their points, quoting proverbs, and offering recipes and remedies. Gemara's legal arguments and traditions are embedded in a compendium rich in stories and fascinating details about the desires, habits, and social structures of human beings in particular cultural settings. These volumes are not designed for giving quick answers, however. Those who yearned for the legal equivalent of crisis intervention had to wait until the post-Talmudic codes were invented (see "What Are Codes?").

Complicating the compilation of the Talmud, a group of later scholars known as the Stammaim (500–700 CE) edited the Babylonian Talmud. They reshaped its discussions and brought rabbis from different times and places into conversation with one another, bringing the text into its present form.

The Orders (Sedarim) of the Mishnah are as follows:

1. *Zeraim (Seeds)*—Laws related to agriculture in Israel, portions of the harvest that go to community sustenance, and laws of blessings

2. *Mo'ed (Holy Times)*—Laws about Shabbat, festivals, and fasts

3. *Nashim (Women)*—Laws about status questions such as marriage and divorce and other matters about women that interest the rabbis

4. *Nezikin (Damages)*—Civil and criminal law, courts, and judicial procedure
5. *Kodashim (Holy Things)*—Laws pertaining to the Temple
6. *Tehorot (Purities)*—Laws of ritual purity and impurity

Appendix E:
What Is Midrash?

MIDRASH (PL. MIDRASHIM) CAN BE translated as "That Which Is Investigated" or "That Which Is Explained." This form of scholarly interpretation of Torah seeks to understand the mysterious, unexplained, and problematic elements of the biblical narrative. The first midrashim were created by the rabbis in 10 CE, and the writing of new midrashim, which has continued pretty much ever since, is still being done today.

There are two varieties of midrash: aggadic and halakhic. Making a hard and fast distinction between the two types is difficult. As many scholars have pointed out, aggadic and halakhic midrash are mutually interdependent and tend to seep into one another. What they have in common is twofold—they both are used to derive new meaning from the text and comment verse by verse on the biblical book in question.

If you are looking for a defined, quick response, halakhic midrash is for you. Halakhic midrash uses the text of the Torah to justify or introduce new rabbinic interpretations of the commandments and sometimes also offers deeper explanations of their meanings. The main collections of this type are *Mekhilta D'Rabbi Yishmael,* which covers Exodus from chapter 12 onward, *Sifra* on Leviticus, *Sifrei Zuta* on Numbers, and *Sifrei* on Deuteronomy.

Aggadic midrash is for you if you are interested in widening your perspective on sacred stories. Suggesting background, context, or motivations for characters' actions, aggadic midrashim are parables that enrich these tantalizing narratives with accounts of what could have been. Scholars have written a great deal about the creative vigor, moral immediacy, and theological power of this form of midrash. Some of these stories have become so well known, in fact, that people do not always realize they are interpretive tales rather than original scripture—the famous account of Avraham as the son of an idol carver who smashes the statues in his father's workshop in an attempt to show him what monotheism is.

The goal of midrash is not to produce one definitive reading of a verse or story but rather a variety of possible readings according to different scholars. A common heading for these alternative commentaries is *davar acher*, meaning "another interpretation." A whole page of these alternatives may be appended to a verse. The reader's job is not to determine which one is right but to view them as pieces of a larger truth. Each teaching may at some time speak to us. Midrashic truth is multivocal, many-voiced. The rabbis assumed that the meanings of the Written Torah are inexhaustible, waiting for us to discover them. One of their favorite sayings is "The Torah has seventy faces." Seventy is the rabbinic way of saying *lots*.

Appendix F:
What Is Halakhah and Why Do Jews Need It?

THE MOST PRECISE TRANSLATION OF the Hebrew word *halakhah* might be "the going" or "the walking" rather than "law." Halakhah is the path-making process by which we transform the Jewish system of meanings and values into action. Judaism asserts that to serve God we must translate what we value into actions, not just prayers or good thoughts: hence, we have halakhah, a process for taking our values on the road. Halakhah addresses the question, What does God (or that-which-is sacred-and-transcends-me) want us to do in this kind of situation? We usually don't think up the answer on the spot. All cultural groups instill into their members a set of religious and ethical rules that order their world and are perceived as just and reasonable. There will always be some people who, when confronted with a juicy opportunity, will respond, "The hell with God, ethics, meaning, and everybody else too! My only concerns are (1) What do I want? and (2) Can I get away with grabbing it?"

But most people are not narcissists or sociopaths. They care about what is right and good, and their relationships with others matter to them. But quandaries come up. In all legal systems, questions occur when people are unsure whether the rules they know apply. Perhaps there are special circumstances. Perhaps conditions have changed so that a rule that worked previously will now cause suffering or injustice. Perhaps an unprecedented situation has arisen for which there doesn't seem to be a rule. These problems happen because human beings and their historical and cultural settings change. To do the right and the good—*ha-tov v'ha-yashar*—in a constantly changing world requires a legal process, a halakhah. Only a process can sustain core values and yet change when justice and compassion require change.

Justice and compassion are obligations because we live in a world with other people and what we do affects them. Halakhic cases are stories. They take place in a specific time and place populated by a cast of characters. Legal philosopher Robert Cover argued that law cannot simply be reduced to a book of regulations. Law is much bigger and more complex than that. Law, Cover wrote, emerges out of a *nomos*, a universe of meaning, and universes of meaning and the values implicit in them are embodied in stories. Judaism's communal stories include the Creation, the history of the People Israel—including enslavement and liberation from Egypt—and the giving of the Torah on Mount Sinai. As the Mishnah points out (*Sanhedrin* 4:5), the creation of Adam (literally "the earthling") as a single individual means that all human beings have one origin; none are superior to others. The story of our slavery grounds many laws against oppressing foreigners or strangers. The story of the giving of the Torah teaches that responsibility is sacred.

These understandings are deeply embedded in our Jewish *nomos*, our universe of meaning. When we are in tune with our *nomos*, we feel responsible to embody our Jewish stories in action. Their many meanings unfold out of our acts, begetting more Jewish stories.

Halakhah, then, is a legal process that embodies centuries upon centuries of Jewish stories and stipulates the responsibilities that flow from them all while allowing for changes in environments and cultural norms and the emergence of previously unknown problems. Applying halakhah to particular cases requires knowing its categories and values and previous cases and rulings while also being able to exercise creativity about fitting what is already known to perhaps unimagined situations.

Being a Jew means being chosen by Jewish stories—either because they were handed down to you or because they called you to them from far away. When you respond to their call, you accept the obligation to embody them in your actions. Spelling out the obligations inherent in these stories is a slippery business, for what you do is never just your personal affair, even if you live on a desert island. Personal business always turns out to be transpersonal, and, for Judaism, personal business is of concern to God as well. Consequently, the question, What ought I do? leads to Judaism's vast collection of stories, books, and arguments. It helps to become familiar with as many of these resources as you can. Find other people who can help you think without being too pushy, since ultimately, it is you who are responsible for what you decide. Probably some of those helpful people will be rabbis.

Being a Jew requires learning your basic obligations and trying to act on them with integrity. But even the simplest "thou shalts" and "thou shalt nots" become complicated when exact definitions, conditions, and contexts need to be specified. That is why halakhah unfolds into a long legal tradition. There are biblical laws, some of which contradict one another in their details. Following the Bible is the Mishnah, a legal compilation that often includes dissenting opinions. Then the Gemara, the later part of the Talmud, asks what exactly the Mishnah meant and in what cases the law applies, evoking more dissenting opinions. After the Talmud, there are layers upon layers of reinterpretation of law, some of them radical reinterpretations. The codes were originally designed as shortcuts. And finally we have the responsa, in which a questioner asks a rabbi or rabbinic committee of experts about unprecedented cases or cases in which existing law creates injustice.

The interactions between multiple levels of text and multiple decisors are complicated. Life is complicated. The universe is complicated. It helps to have a path, one that is informed by a tradition with its universe of meaning embodied in stories, and a community that shares a common vocabulary of stories and ways to put them into action. That way, you, too, become a path maker; as the Spanish poem by Antonio Machado puts it, "The path is made by walking."

Appendix G:
What Are Codes?

CODES EMERGED IN THE SIXTH to tenth centuries CE as collections of rabbinic rulings, designed to serve communities who had immediate need of concise, clear guidance. While the first codes were assembled by some of the Geonim (the post-Talmudic legal authorities), and an early eleventh century compendium by Rabbi Issac Alfasi (known as the RIF) exists, the first of the great legal codes was composed in the eleventh century by Rabbi Moshe ben Maimon, often known by his initials as the Rambam or Maimonides.

By the eleventh century, Jews had settled all over the Middle East and throughout parts of Europe. What had once been Israel had fallen to one conqueror after another since the Roman Empire, most of them inhospitable to Jewish inhabitants. Many places throughout the Middle East and North Africa became perilous when Islam entered its most militant missionary phase, although by the tenth century some Islamic countries permitted Jewish and Christian minorities under the *dhimmi* laws that allotted these groups some rights but extra taxes. Christian countries were also unwelcoming, at worst offering a choice between conversion or death and at best, ghettoization, heavy surtaxes, and special identifying insignia or garments such as the yellow star.

Most of these Jewish settlements did not have access to scholar experts, who had the skills to process all these legal materials, nor did the little communities have access to the huge stacks of handwritten reference books, each of which cost a mint. Even after the invention of the printing press (ca. 1440) when the first printed codes (1476) and Talmud tractates (1483) became available, Rambam's creation of the *Mishneh Torah*, a digest of laws neatly indexed and arranged in logical order the way Aristotle might have organized them, was an elegant solution. The Greek-influenced organization of the subject matter was particularly revolutionary. Classical Greek knowledge had just been rediscovered in the sophisticated Islamic world, and Rambam was a big fan. Eventually the Greek revival spread to the less civilized West as well, and codification became the latest innovation, even in the wilds of Europe and Britain.

The *Mishneh Torah* made a much smaller and hence more convenient, more portable, and cheaper collection of books than the Talmud. You easily found your topic, and Rambam gave you a brief overview and a quick legal decision: permitted or forbidden, and sometimes a penalty as well. Many scholars hated the *Mishneh Torah*. As they pointed out, all this simplicity and accessibility had a downside. You lost the rich complexity of Talmudic discussion that valued many voices instead of a single authoritative voice. Moreover, Maimonides did not provide citations. Researchers could not look up the sources if they didn't already know them. Hence, while the *Mishneh*

Torah made the process of legal decision making much easier, the results were also less nuanced and more authoritarian.

Rambam was, of course, a Sephardic scholar. He was born in Spain but fled for his life to Egypt. Consequently his code reflects Sephardic custom. But subsequently, both Ashkenazic and Sephardic rabbis wrote codes: for example, Rabbi Asher Ben Yechiel, a.k.a. the ROSH (ca. thirteenth century), and Rabbi Ya'akov ben Asher, a.k.a. the Tur, so named after his code the *Arbah Turim*, meaning "the Four Columns" (thirteenth to fourteenth centuries).

The second great major codifier after Maimonides, however, was Rabbi Yosef Karo (1488–1575), who composed first the *Beit Yosef* and then the *Shulchan Arukh* ("the Set Table"). This work reflected Sephardic practice and incorporated the decisions of Rambam, the ROSH, and other authorities. Shortly after, Rabbi Moshe Isserles, known as the Rema (1525–72), wrote a commentary on the *Shulchan Arukh* citing Ashkenazic divergences from Sephardic practice and named it *Ha-Mappah* ("the Tablecloth"). In doing so, the Rema made the *Shulchan Arukh* a universal resource because it included the practices of East and West. Ever since, all editions of the *Shulchan Arukh* have incorporated the commentary of the Rema.

Jewish legal codes continue to be written to this very day. Ironically, all the dissident voices the first codes tried to silence have crept back up in the form of commentaries in columns running the length and breadth of the outer perimeter of every page, including restoring the equivalent of footnotes to the primary sources. Two conclusions can be drawn: (1) the question of how a Jew ought to act to fulfill the divine will in particular contexts and situations is as important now as it ever was and (2) telling Jews what to do is no easier now than it was in earlier eras.

Appendix H:
Timeline of the Jewish World

JEWISH TIME EXTENDS OVER THREE millennia and many places, but it does not happen in a vacuum. Some secular events have been added to this timeline as signposts. They will help orient people unfamiliar with Jewish history. The signposts are also reminders that events in secular history had profound impacts on Jewish communities and their habitats.

What Do We Mean by BCE and CE?

The terms BC ("before Christ") and AD (anno Domini—"the year of our Lord") were introduced by Christian scholars around the year 500 of the Common Era (AD) so that the birth of Jesus of Nazareth would be the central point of historical orientation through which past and present is viewed.

Religion scholars and educated Jews prefer the more neutral language BCE ("before the Common Era") and CE ("of the Common Era"). These are the terms we use here. The small *ca.* before a date is the abbreviation for the Latin *circa*, meaning "around" or "approximately."

Timeline of the Jewish World

ca. 1400–1200 BCE: The tribes of Israel come into existence.

ca. 1000 BCE: David conquers Jerusalem and reigns over a united kingdom of the twelve tribes of Israel.

ca. 959 BCE: The First Temple in Jerusalem is founded, built during King Solomon's reign.

930 BCE: The united kingdom of Israel splits into the Southern Kingdom of Judah, encompassing the tribes of Judah, Benjamin, and Levi and ruled over by the House of David, and the Northern Kingdom of Israel, encompassing the ten other tribes and ruled by no consistent dynasty.

772 BCE: The Assyrian king Sargon II conquers the Northern Kingdom of Israel and enslaves and deports the overwhelming majority of its inhabitants. They are called the Ten Lost Tribes and are never heard of again. The remnants left in the Land of Israel are absorbed and assimilated into the Southern Kingdom of Judah.

587 BCE: The Babylonian king Nebuchadnezzar sacks Jerusalem and destroys the Holy Temple. The following year, the Babylonians deport many Judaeans to Babylonia. This is the beginning of the Babylonian Exile (Galut Bavel).

539 BCE: Having conquered the Babylonians, the Persian emperor Cyrus the Great decrees that Judaeans in Babylonia may return to Judah and rebuild the city of Jerusalem and the Holy Temple.

332 BCE: Alexander the Great conquers the Land of Israel. Because his policy is not to interfere with local cultures and religions, he is a popular ruler.

200 BCE–200 CE: The canonization of the Hebrew Bible, the Tanakh, takes place.

167–160 BCE: The Maccabean Revolt against the Seleucid Empire and its Hellenistic attempt to erase Jewish religious practice takes place.

30–6 BCE: Rome annexes Judea (which is Judah plus part of the old Northern Kingdom) and assumes authority over it amid continuing unrest.

30–20 BCE: The Pharisaic academies of Hillel and Shammai are established, and Rabbinic Judaism begins.

ca. 4–6 CE: Jesus of Nazareth is born.

70: Roman generals Vespasian and his son Titus destroy the city of Jerusalem and the Second Temple. Rabbi Yochanan ben Zakkai founds the great rabbinic academy at Yavneh.

75–100: Josephus (b. Yosef ben Mattityahu, a.k.a Flavius Josephus), the impassioned, controversial (and sole) historian of our people's history from 300 BCE to 100 CE, completes *The Wars of the Jews, Antiquities of the Jews, Against Apion,* and *The Life of Flavius Josephus.*

ca. 2nd century: Beruriah, a Talmudic scholar, lives. Talmudic tractates identify her as the daughter of Rabbi Hananya ben Tradyon and the wife of Rabbi Meir.

132–135: Shimon Bar Kochba leads the last great (but unsuccessful) Jewish rebellion against Rome. In retribution, the emperor Hadrian orders a massive purge resulting in the martyrdom of many of the greatest rabbis of the age, including Rabbi Akiva. The Romans change the name of the province from Judea to Syria Palaestina and Jerusalem to Aelia Capitolina.

200: Rabbi Yehudah Ha-Nasi (Judah the Prince) oversees the final redaction of the Mishnah.

327: The Roman emperor Constantine converts to Christianity and makes it the official religion of the Roman Empire. Persecution of Jews in the Roman Empire increases in the extreme.

ca. 367: The twenty-seven books that make up the Christian New Testament are completed.

400: The Palestinian Talmud gets its final redaction.

476: The Roman Empire in the West falls. The Byzantine Empire in the East continues to flourish.

550–750: The Babylonian Talmud gets its final redaction.

ca. 580–632: The life of the prophet Muhammad and the establishment of Islam take place.

600–1050: This spans the period of the Geonim—the scholars of the great Babylonian rabbinic academies.

990–1055: The Umayyad Muslim king of Granada, Spain, appoints the Jewish diplomat, general, poet, linguist, and biblical scholar Shmuel ibn Nagrela (known as Shmuel ha-Nagid) to be vizier of the kingdom, ushering in a high culture of arts, literature, and prosperity among Sephardic Jews.

1040–1105: The commentator Rabbi Shlomo Yitzchaki of Troyes, France, known as Rashi, lives. He was the sine qua non of textual commentators whose commentaries on Tanakh and Talmud are always included with the text.

1078: Pope Gregory VIII prohibits Jews from holding offices in Christian lands. In the following centuries, Christian rulers systematically prohibit Jews from land ownership and most trades and crafts, relegating them largely to small tenant farming, limited merchant trade, and money-lending. Special taxes are levied on Jews.

1095–1272: The nine Christian Crusades, responsible for the atrocious massacres of tens of thousands of Jews both in Europe and the Middle East, take place. Along with Muslims, who occupied the Holy Land and claimed it as part of their own sacred history, the Jews were classified as enemies of God and were systematically targeted for slaughter.

1138–1204: Rabbi Moshe ben Maimon, known as Maimonides and Rambam, legal scholar and philosopher par excellence, lives. His *Mishneh Torah* (1170–80), the first of the Jewish legal codes, is published.

1170–96: Dulcie of Worms (wife of Rabbi Eleazar) lives. She becomes a learned pietist and one of the first female prayer leaders (*firzogerins*). Her business acumen independently supported her family and her husband's many students.

1240–1305: Rabbi Moshe ben ShemTov de Leon lives. He leads a circle of mystics in Spain, with whom he composes what becomes the core text of Jewish mysticism, the Zohar.

1270–1340: Rabbi Ya'akov ben Asher lives. His legal code *Arbah Turim* (commonly called the *Tur*) sets the format for all future legal codes and is the second of the three greatest Jewish legal codes.

1480–92: The Spanish Inquisition is established, culminating in the Kingdom of Spain expelling all Jewish residents who refuse baptism. If discovered, baptized Jews who practice Judaism in secret are burned alive publicly in autos-da-fé.

16th century: Francesca Sarah, scholar, maggid, and visionary, lives sometime during this century. She is the center of a circle of female mystics in Sfat. She is described in Chaim Vital's *Sefer Ha-Chezyonot* and Tirzah Firestone's *The Receiving.*

1517: Martin Luther posts the Ninety-Five Theses, provoking the Protestant Reformation. Luther also goes on to write "On the Jews and Their Lies," one of the first modern anti-Semitic tracts.

1525–1609: Rabbi Yitzchak Luria (known as the ARI) lives. He institutes a number of customs that still survive—such as the Kabbalat Shabbat prayer service on Friday evenings and dressing in white for the Shabbat—and teaches profoundly innovative mystical theologies that have affected numerous Jewish movements ever since.

1563: Rabbi Yosef Karo, a Sephardic legal scholar and mystic, publishes the *Shulchan Arukh* ("the Set Table"), the third of the three most significant Jewish legal codes.

1571: Rabbi Moshe Isserles publishes his commentary on the *Shulchan Arukh, Ha-Mappah* ("the Tablecloth"), adding Ashkenazic legal decisions that differ from the Sephardic norms.

1626–76: Shabbetai Tzvi, a false messiah, lives. His actions send shock waves of chaos through the Jewish world, profoundly affecting Jewish movements for the next two centuries at least.

1646–1724: Glückel of Hameln lives. Her social and business activities span Germany, France, Denmark, Holland, Austria, and Poland. Her memoirs, written toward the end of the Thirty Years War, detail what it is like to be a Jew in Western Europe during that time.

1648–49: In Ukraine and Poland, Cossacks led by Bohdan Khmelnytsky engage in a brutal series of massacres of the Jews, killing at least twenty thousand and causing many more to flee, who often experienced dire poverty, starvation, or slavery. The effects of the massacres haunt Jewish life in those areas for over two centuries.

1654: The first Jewish community is established in North America, as twenty-three Sephardic Jews arrive in New Amsterdam from Portuguese Brazil.

1698–1760: Rabbi Yisrael ben Eliezer, known as the Ba'al Shem Tov ("Good Master of the [Holy] Name") or the Besht, lives. Born in Ukraine, he travels, learning Kabbalah and gaining a reputation as a wonder-worker and saintly teacher. He settles in the small town of Medzhybizh, Ukraine, where he founds the populist ecstatic movement known as Chasidism.

1720–97: Eliyahu ben Shlomo Zalman, known as the Gaon of Vilna, lives. A child prodigy of remarkable ability, he becomes one of the greatest scholars of Talmud, halakhah, and Kabbalah.

1729–86: Moses Mendelssohn, the first secular Jewish scholar, lives. He begins to introduce the Enlightenment to European Jewry, with predictably mixed results. For some Jews, he is considered the first modern Jewish intellectual. For others, he is an arch-heretic.

1745–1812: Rebbe Schneur Zalman of Liady, founder of Chabad Chasidim, lives. An accomplished scholar and halakhist, he creates a Chasidic siddur and legal code titled the *Rav Shulchan Arukh*, as well as a classic of Jewish mysticism, *Likutei Amaraim*, commonly called the *Tanya*.

1762–1839: Rabbi Moshe Schreiber, or Moshe Sofer, lives. Known by the name of his magnum opus, the *Chatam Sofer*, he is an

absolute and uncompromising opponent to Enlightenment sec-
ularism and the budding Reform movement. Punning on a verse
from the Mishnah concerning first fruits (*chadash*), he famously
declares, "*Kol chadash asur min ha-Torah*" (Anything new is forbidden by the Torah). He becomes the founder of what is today
Haredi (ultra-Orthodox) Judaism.

1772–1810: Rebbe Nachman of Breslov, the deeply charismatic, ecstatic
founder of the Breslover Chasidic community, lives. He creates
Kabbalistic parables of extraordinary complexity and beauty,
such as *The Seven Beggars*, and the philosophical work *Likutei
Moharan*. His theology—now known as the Breslover school—
emphasizes intimate connection to God and private contemplation.

1780–1852: Malkah of Belz, wife of Shalom Rokeach, the Belzer Rebbe,
and matriarch of the Belzer dynasty, lives in Ukraine. She is
known to have been a holy woman and for the joy with which
she held court, her amazing healing powers, and her wise counsel
throughout the community.

1781: The American Revolution, desperate for funding, secures critical
fundraising aid from Haym Solomon, whose multilingual fluency
allows him to act as an intermediary agent from the Continental
Congress and army to France, Prussia, and other foreign powers.

1790: United States President George Washington writes a letter to
the Jewish community of Newport, Rhode Island, in response to
their well wishes, in which he proclaims America to be a place
of tolerance and religious liberty, specifically welcoming and
including Jews.

1791: In the wake of the French Revolution, French Jews are given
full citizenship for the first time since the fall of the Roman
Empire: in exchange, the French Jewish communities indicate
they will be loyal to the French state. Over the course of the next
several decades, virtually all Western European countries grant
enfranchisement to Jews in exchange for promises of primary
loyalty to the nation-state.

1791: The Russian tsar confines all Jews under Russian rule to the Pale of Settlement, a zone from the Baltic to Black Sea, encompassing what is today Lithuania, Latvia, Poland, Ukraine, Belarus, Moldova, and a small sliver of Russia. Jewish males as young as twelve are frequently forcibly conscripted into the tsar's army for twenty- or thirty-year terms of service, laws are passed restricting Jews from various opportunities and professions, and pogroms are not only tolerated but often actively encouraged by authorities.

1807: French emperor Napoleon, intrigued by Jewish law, attempts to convene a French Sanhedrin. The attempt is largely unsuccessful, as virtually nobody accepts the authority of the French Sanhedrin in any matter of religious law, though few communities object seriously to the so-called Grand Sanhedrin's declaration that French Jews will be loyal to Napoleon and France.

1808–88: Rabbi Samson Raphael Hirsch lives. He and another German rabbi-scholar, Azriel Hildesheimer, found a school of thought based on the maxim *"Torah im Derech Eretz"* (Torah study along with secular study). This movement becomes today's Modern Orthodoxy.

1810–20: The Reform movement is established in Germany, and rabbis such as Leopold Zunz and Abraham Geiger begin innovating Jewish practice. The reforms attempt to reshape Judaism as an Enlightenment religion, suitable for secularly educated citizens of modern nation-states. Traditionalist reactions to the rise of the Reform movement include what has evolved into Modern Orthodoxy and today's Haredi (or ultra-Orthodox) communities.

1815–1905: Hannah Rachel of Ludomir—scholar, sage, teacher, and miracle worker—lives. Excommunicated by the rabbis in her native region, she makes aliyah at age fifty-five and continues her work in Eretz Yisrael.

1856–1941: Louis D. Brandeis, the first Jew to sit on the United States Supreme Court, lives. As a lawyer, he represents ordinary citizens against corporate interests and helps to develop a right to privacy. He also helps create the Federal Reserve System and Federal Trade Commission.

1860–1904: Theodor Herzl, the father of modern Zionism, lives. Herzl vocally agitates for establishing a Jewish State in the historic Jewish homeland. He convened the first World Zionist Congress, which became an annual event. Herzl envisions the future Jewish State as a socialist utopia, and the initial waves of immigration under Ottoman Turkish and then British rule are largely secular Socialist Jews.

1860–1945: Henrietta Szold, educator, scholar, social activist, and community organizer, lives. During Szold's twenty-three years at the Jewish Publication Society, the publisher produces many of its most notable works of major scholarship. After a transformative trip to Israel, she makes aliyah and founds Hadassah (now one of the largest NGOs in the world), which transforms medical care in British Palestine. Through her subsequent government work, Szold also leads the development of the country's social work system. Szold goes on to serve as director of Youth Aliyah, an organization that saves eleven thousand young people from Europe during World War II and the surrounding years.

1865–1935: Rabbi Avraham Yitzchak Ha-Kohen Kook lives. His family had roots both in Chasidism and the Lithuanian yeshiva movement, and he studies both. An ardent Zionist, he makes aliyah in 1904 to become the chief rabbi of Yafo. In 1921 he is appointed Ashkenazi chief rabbi of Palestine.

1875: Isaac Mayer Wise, a leading Reform rabbi in America, founds Hebrew Union College in Cincinnati.

1879–1955: Albert Einstein lives. Born to a secular Jewish family, Einstein becomes the greatest physicist since Isaac Newton. A staunch Zionist, he is offered the first presidency of the State of Israel when it is established but politely declines.

1881: Jewish Socialist labor activist Samuel Gompers founds the Federation of Organized Trades and Labor Unions, the forerunner of the American Federation of Labor. Gompers was one of many Jewish American organizers, a list that includes Rose Schneiderman, Pauline Newman, Clara Lemlich, and Fannia Cohn.

1881–1983: Rabbi Mordecai Kaplan lives. Born in Lithuania, he comes to New York as a young boy and lives there until his death. Originally ordained as an Orthodox rabbi, he receives a doctorate from Columbia University. Finding Orthodoxy untenable, Kaplan develops the philosophical basis of Reconstructionist Judaism. He saw Judaism as a civilization rather than merely a religion and posited a God who is a cosmic process rather than a Thou. In 1968, he and his son-in-law and chief student, Ira Eisenstein, found Reconstructionist Rabbinical College, and the Reconstructionist movement separates from Conservative Judaism.

1886–1973: David Ben-Gurion lives. He is a brilliant Zionist leader and statesman who becomes the first prime minister of the State of Israel in 1948.

1894–1917: The secret police of the last tsar of Russia, Nicholas II, create and release an anti-Semitic pamphlet, *The Protocols of the Learned Elders of Zion*, a pamphlet purporting to be a collection of found documents revealing a gigantic Jewish conspiracy to control the world. *The Protocols of the Learned Elders of Zion* and works that draw on it become core texts for modern anti-Semitic organizations, from Nazis and the Ku Klux Klan to white supremacist and radical Islamist groups today.

1898–1978: Golda Meir lives. Born in Kiev and raised in Milwaukee, Wisconsin, she emigrates to British Palestine in 1924. Meir quickly becomes a leader in the Histadrut (the national Jewish trade union in Israel) and then heads the Jewish Agency for Israel's political department. She is a member of the provisional government established at Israel's independence in 1948. In 1969 Meir becomes Israel's prime minister.

1907–72: Rabbi Abraham Joshua Heschel lives. One of the greatest modern Jewish philosophers, Heschel comes from a distinguished Chasidic dynasty. In addition to a private Orthodox ordination, he has a liberal ordination as well as a doctorate from the University of Berlin. He leaves Europe in 1938 weeks before Germany invades Poland. Heschel's philosophy and theology are deeply influenced by Chasidic teachings about joy and awe. Heschel's life models ethical commitment. He attends the Second Vatican Council, lobbying for reforms of anti-Semitic church teachings and liturgy. He supports the civil rights movement, marching with Dr. Martin Luther King Jr., and protests the war in Vietnam.

1909: Tel Aviv is founded as a Hebrew-speaking Jewish city. The first kibbutz is also founded in northern Israel at Deganya.

1911: A fire in the Triangle Shirtwaist Factory in New York takes the lives of 146 workers. They cannot escape because the stairwell doors are locked during workers' shifts. The victims are mostly Jewish and Italian immigrant women, ages fourteen to forty-six. In the aftermath, the International Ladies' Garment Workers' Union gains members and influence.

1917: British Foreign Minister Lord Arthur Balfour issues a letter on behalf of the government to the Jewish community indicating that His Majesty's government favors the creation of a Jewish State in Palestine. This Balfour Declaration is the first time a major power has lent support to the Zionist cause.

1920: The Nazi Party founded.

1921–24: The United States institutes several immigration laws restricting the admittance of Jews into the United States.

1923: In the unsuccessful Beer Hall Putsch, Nazis attempt to take over Munich. They fail miserably, and Adolf Hitler is imprisoned. While in prison, he writes *Mein Kampf*. The Nazi Party founds their newspaper, *Der Sturmer*.

1924: Hillel House is founded at the University of Illinois. It eventually becomes the indispensable Jewish organization on every major college campus (and many minor ones) in the United States.

1925: Hebrew University is founded in Jerusalem.

1933: Adolf Hitler becomes chancellor of Germany. Jews in America and Britain begin boycotting German goods. The Vatican accepts Nazis as a legitimate authority in Germany.

1933: Rose Schneiderman becomes the sole woman President Franklin D. Roosevelt appoints to the National Labor Advisory Board. She rewrites labor codes for every industry with a predominantly female work force.

1934: Jewish baseball superstar Hank Greenberg refuses to play on Yom Kippur.

1935: Nazis pass the Nuremberg Laws, making anti-Semitism the core law of the land. Jews are stripped of their rights.

1935: Regina Jonas, a liberal (Reform) scholar, is ordained privately in Germany. She is believed to be the first female rabbi.

1938: In America, Charles Coughlin, a Catholic priest, begins a national anti-Semitic media campaign. The German American Bund sponsors a pro-Nazi rally at Madison Square Garden and one hundred thousand attend. On November 9 in Germany, Kristallnacht, a major pogrom, is executed by the Nazis.

1939: Germany invades Poland, beginning World War II.

1940: The first trains arrive at Auschwitz. The death camp is part of a systematic plan of genocide, eventually termed the "Final Solution to the Jewish Problem." During the course of the war, some six million Jews—about one-third of the world's Jewish population at the time—are killed in death camps, ghettos, massacres, and other acts. This unprecedented slaughter is called the Shoah, or Holocaust.

1941: At least thirty-four thousand Jewish men, women, and children—some say perhaps as many as one hundred thousand—are massacred at Babi Yar, just outside Kiev in Ukraine. It is one of the worst massacres of the Shoah.

1944: Britain forms the Jewish Brigade of the Royal Army, utilizing volunteers from Jewish communities in British Palestine. Veterans will later constitute a critical core of the Haganah forces during the Israeli War of Independence and the founders of the Israel Defense Forces.

1945: World War II ends. The Allies hold war-crime trials at Nuremberg for Nazi leaders, employing the newly coined word *genocide*, and innovating the terminology of "crimes against humanity." The United Nations is established, headquartered in New York City.

1946: The conflict between the Jewish underground freedom fighters and the British authorities in Palestine intensifies dramatically as Britain drags its feet on establishing a Jewish State.

1947: Britain announces its intentions to partition Mandatory Palestine into two states, one Jewish and one Arab. The United Nations adopts Resolution 181, calling for Palestine to be partitioned into a Jewish and an Arab state. The proposal is accepted by Jewish leaders, under the auspices of David Ben-Gurion, who manages to secure virtually unanimous Jewish willingness to accept the plan. The proposal is rejected by the Arab Higher Committee for Palestine.

1948: David Ben-Gurion leads an assembly of Jewish leaders in Tel Aviv where the inception of the independent State of Israel is declared. All surrounding Arab powers immediately declare war and advance troops against the Jewish forces. US President Harry S. Truman recognizes the State of Israel within one hour of its declaration. The Soviet Union soon follows suit. The War of Independence lasts until 1949, when cease-fires (but not peace treaties) are agreed with the Arab nations. Wars will occur regularly for the next thirty years, all of them won by Israel, but unresolved political and social issues will continue to plague Israel and Palestine through the present time. Over the next four years, the Arab nations of the Middle East expel the majority of their Jewish populace, sometimes clearing out communities that had existed for thousands of years: over eight hundred thousand Mizrahi (Middle Eastern and North African) Jews flood into

Israel, shifting the balance of the Jewish population away from its previous heavy Ashkenazi majority.

Reader, you are invited to go on from here.

Glossary

Abaye: Nachmani ben Kaylil, head of the Babylonian academy in Pumbedita in the fourth century CE. Hundreds of debates between Abaye and Rava (head of Mechoza academy) are cited in the Talmud.

acosmism: A mystical belief that nothing exists but God. The entire cosmos is a part of God rather than consisting of entities distinct from God. Acosmism would deny the existence of Otherness.

amora (pl. amoraim): A teacher and interpreter of Mishnah in one of the learning academies of Babylonia or Palestine between the mid-fourth century to beginning of the sixth century. Their work is recorded in the Talmud. See "What Is the Talmud?"

***apikoros* (pl. *apikorsim*):** A nonbeliever or heretic.

Bedtime Shema: Blessings to say before going to sleep, including the declaration of the Divine unity and prayers for protection.

***bensch gomel*:** To recite the Birkat HaGomel prayer of gratitude after surviving a serious danger.

***bittul ha-yesh* ("self-nullification"):** Chasidic ideal of transcendence (cleaving to God, or *devekut*), attained by self-abnegation and humility.

Book of Life (Sefer HaChayim): A central metaphor of the Days of Awe. The early rabbis, many of whom were scribes, envisioned God as a scribe inscribing the names of the deserving in a book that lists those who will live in the new year.

Buber, Martin (1878–1965): Philosopher and educator born in Vienna, author of *I and Thou* (1923), which introduced the concept of relationship (with God and also with other people) as an encounter between two "thous," where each is completely open to and present with the other. He also founded the National Jewish Committee, made aliyah to Eretz Yisrael, and taught philosophy at Hebrew University of Jerusalem.

Chasidism: A charismatic Jewish movement founded in the eighteenth century emphasizing piety and joy. See "Timeline of the Jewish World."

chavruta: A learning partner for Jewish text study, which is usually dialogic.

Chumash with Rashi: The Five Books of Moses published with commentary by Rashi (medieval commentator par excellence).

daven: To pray.

d'var Torah (pl. divrei Torah): A brief teaching on a passage from Torah. Any Jew might be called on to offer a d'var Torah at a service, or at a Shabbat or festival table, or during study. We all have Torah to teach one another.

Eikha: The book of Lamentations in the Hebrew Bible, chanted on Tisha B'Av.

Eruvin **(Mixtures):** A tractate of *Seder Moed* in Talmud that concerns the boundaries that delineate the physical domains of travel and carrying objects on Shabbat.

Etz Chayim (Tree of Life): This image, describing Lady Wisdom in Proverbs 3:18, is appropriated by the rabbis to refer to the Torah. *Etz Chayim* is also the title of the Conservative Movement's one-volume Five Books of Moses with Haftarot, prophetic readings and commentary. For more about the importance of tree symbolism in Judaism, see Tu B'Shevat in "The Cycle of the Jewish Year."

food blessings: The sages of Jewish tradition considered the saying of one hundred blessings a day to be ideal. Blessings over wine, bread, fruit, vegetables, grains, and other foods offer ample opportunity to do this. Blessings can also be said over natural phenomena such as thunder, lightning, rainbows, the ocean, or blossoming trees. Blessings express both appreciation for personal benefits and a sense of wonder.

gabbai (m.), gabba'it (f.) (Aramaic): An assistant to a great teacher. Also, in the synagogue, the one who aids and announces the Torah readers, rolls the scroll to the proper place, and is responsible for other preparations for the service.

***G'mar chatimah tovah* ("May your seal be a good one"):** A greeting said on Yom Kippur. A wish that the person being addressed, whose inscription in the Book of Life for the coming year is tentative on Rosh HaShanah, will have that inscription decisively sealed on Yom Kippur.

***Ha-Chovel*:** The chapter of *Bava Kamma* (part of Talmud, *Tractate Nezikin*) that discusses five types of restitution for personal injury. These forms of monetary compensation constitute the rabbinic understanding of the biblical legal category "an eye for an eye."

Hallel: A component of the morning service during festivals and Rosh Chodesh consisting of Psalms 113–117, many of which open with the exclamation "Hallelujah—let all praise God." Their theme is gratitude for rescue by God.

***ha-rishonim* ("the first authorities"):** The postrabbinic commentators who emerged after the end of the Babylonian Talmud academies (eleventh century) through the fifteenth century.

Havdalah ("distinction"): A weekly ceremony using a braided candle, wine, and spices that marks the end of Shabbat and the beginning of the working week. Havdalah is both the parallel and opposite of Kiddush.

***hitlahavut* (from *lahav*, "a flame"):** A state of spiritual ecstasy during prayer, associated with Chasidic practice.

I and Thou: The central concept of Martin Buber's most influential philosophic work, *I and Thou* (1923), proposes a full-on meeting with the Other, in which we commune with integrity and wholeness. This idea suggests the opposite of "I-It," or transactional relationships where we are using the other person for some purpose of our own. I-Thou refers to our relationship with God, which models our encounters with people. Buber saw the task of human beings as transforming the I-It world into an I-Thou world. See also Buber, Martin.

Ibn Ezra, Abraham (1092–1167): Spanish-born poet and biblical commentator.

Kabbalah (adj. Kabbalistic): Jewish mysticism.

Kaddish: A prayer praising God recited in Aramaic and requiring a quorum of ten Jews, or a minyan.

kavanah **("directed intention"):** A state of focus and devotion during prayer.

Kiddush: A toast over wine before the evening and midday Shabbat or festival meals, praising God for the sacred occasion.

King David: Warrior and poet-king of Israel ca. 1000 BCE. Many of the Psalms are attributed to him.

Kohelet: The book of Ecclesiastes in the Hebrew Bible, traditionally read during the festival of Sukkot.

lifnim mi-shurat ha-din: The Talmudic ethical doctrine that encourages us to go beyond the legal minimum required.

Lurianic Kabbalah: A school of Jewish mysticism named after its founder, Rabbi Isaac Luria (1534–72). See "What Is Jewish Mysticism?"

Ma'ariv ("evening appears"): The evening prayer service.

metzar: A narrow place, tight spot, or dangerous situation.

mezzuzot **("doorposts"):** Small containers holding parchments inscribed with the Shema and other verses from Deuteronomy 6:4–9 and 11:13–21 that Jews affix to their doorposts and entranceways. They are meant as a sign that the inhabitants of this home are Jews who care about serving God.

midat ha-din: God's attribute of strict judgment.

midat ha-rachamim: God's attribute of compassion, which mitigates strict judgment.

Mikra'ot Gedolot (Great Scriptures): The published edition of the Hebrew Bible that includes the Hebrew and Aramaic scriptural text with Masoretic notation and medieval commentaries (first printed by Daniel Bomberg in 1524 in Italy).

Mincha ("offering"): The afternoon prayer service.

minyan: A quorum of ten Jews (originally men but now, in every denomination but Orthodox, Jews of any gender) who must be present for Torah to be read or special prayers, such as Kaddish, to be recited.

Moshe Rabbenu (Moses, our teacher): This is the way the rabbis referred to Moses, and this expression is still favored among Jews. What is valued most about him is not his unique status as lawgiver or special confidante of God but his work at helping others to understand what is right and good.

Musaf ("additional"): The additional morning service on Shabbat and Yom Tov in Conservative and Orthodox liturgies.

mystic: A person who studies and practices mysticism.

***nebach* (Yiddish):** "Alas, What a pity!"

nechemta: A statement of comfort and hope following a rebuke or a harsh text. The rabbis forbid ending any public reading of the Bible on a note of despair. This practice is extended to include sermons and divrei Torah as well. A reader or teacher must not cause people to despair of God's love or help.

Olam Ha-Ba (The World to Come): The afterlife. The rabbis of the Talmud speculate little on what Olam Ha-Ba is and frown upon calculating when the ultimate redemption will occur. One of the few descriptions, *Berakhot* 17a, depicts it as a world of pure contemplation.

oved kochavim: An idolator. Literally, "one who worships the stars." Idolatry means making an image that one understands and believes one can control rather than worshiping a God who cannot be reduced to an image and who is infinitely complex and beyond human control. Idolatry is forbidden by Judaism.

***Perek Shirah* (Chapter of Song):** A medieval text whose premise is that everything prays: stars, stones, birds, animals—all God's creations praise their creator. Accordingly *Perek Shirah* assigns every entity a verse of Psalms or other biblical texts most appropriate to it as its distinctive prayer of praise.

Pesach: The festival of Passover, called the "time of our freedom," which celebrates our redemption from slavery as the biblical book of Exodus narrates. See "The Cycle of the Jewish Year."

piyyut (pl. piyyutim; from Greek, "poet"): Ornate Hebrew liturgical poems. The first such poems date from sixth or seventh centuries CE, but they continued to be written for hundreds of years. They are playful, using acrostics, biblical and midrashic allusions, and other forms of wordplay. Rambam hated them, but he was not noted for his sense of humor or love of poetry.

Rabbi Eliezer (1st and 2nd centuries CE): Eliezer ben Hyrcanus, Talmudic sage of the Tannaitic generation and husband of Imma Shalom.

Rabbi Meir (second century CE): Palestinian sage, scholar, student of Rabbi Akiva, participant in the Bar Kochba revolt, and husband of Beruriah.

rebbe: A beloved teacher or spiritual leader. Also a revered leader of a Chasidic group.

Resh Lakish (200–275 CE): Rabbi Simeon ben Lakish, Talmudic sage reputed to have been a master thief or gladiator in his sinful youth.

responsum: A rabbinic or scholarly letter responding to a question of Jewish practice and halakhah.

Rosenzweig, Franz (1886–1929): Philosopher and educator, founder of the Lehrhaus center for adult Jewish study in Frankfurt, author of *The Star of Redemption,* and cotranslator of the Hebrew Bible into German with Martin Buber.

Rosh Chodesh: A festival celebrating the beginning of the new Jewish month. Musaf and Hallel are added to the morning service. Since Talmudic times, women have traditionally had their own distinctive Rosh Chodesh practices.

seder (pl. sedarim): Seder, meaning "order," has several usages. It could refer to one of the six orders of the Mishnah or to the home service at the Pesach table. Siddur, a prayer book, is another word derived from this Hebrew root meaning "order."

Sefirot: The ten realms of Divine being through which the mystic ascends in order to know God. See also Tree of Sefirot.

***se'udah shlishit* ("third meal"):** The highly spiritual and contemplative final meal eaten on Shabbat and holy days shortly before sunset is associated with anticipating the redemption of the world.

Seventeenth of Tammuz: A fast day in the Jewish calendar that commemorates the breaching of the walls of Jerusalem and the beginning of the three weeks leading up to Tisha B'Av.

Shabbat: A core Jewish observance that marks God's rest after six days of creation. Shabbat observance begins on Friday at sundown and ends on Saturday night at dark. On this day, Jews abstain from specified forms of work and participate in special worship services and an array of home practices, such as candle lighting on Friday evening, partaking of special meals, singing at the table, storytelling, and studying.

Shacharit: The morning prayer service. On Monday, Thursday, and Saturday, this includes a public Torah reading. Mondays and Thursdays were chosen for Torah reading because in the ancient and medieval worlds they were market days, so even rural Jews were likely to have assembled in a large enough town to have a minyan, the quorum of ten required for Torah reading.

Shaddai (also, El Shaddai): This name of God from the Hebrew Bible is associated with Divine protection, which is why the covers of *mezzuzot* are often decorated with the letter *shin*, the first letter of the word *Shaddai*.

Shefa: In Jewish mysticism, a term referring to the flow of Divine influence and abundance.

Shekhinah: God's immanence (as opposed to transcendence) that we encounter through lived experience. In post-Talmudic mystical literature this aspect of God is imaged as feminine.

Shevirat Ha-Kelim (Breaking of the Vessels): In Lurianic Kabbalah, the cosmic catastrophe that occurred at the creation of the world and caused the fragmentation of the Divine essence.

Shiv'a D'Nechemta: Seven Haftarot, or prophetic readings, of consolation read in synagogue during the seven weeks between Tisha B'Av and Rosh HaShanah. See "The Cycle of the Jewish Year."

shlita: The Hebrew acronym for "May [he/she] live a good long life," often said after the name of a prominent living rabbi or teacher (such as the Holy Mysticat). After the death of a holy person, instead of *shlita*, we add *zal* or *z"l*, short for *Zikhrono* or *Zikhronah li'vrakhah*, meaning "May his/her memory be a blessing."

Shulchan Arukh ("the Set Table"): One of the most authoritative legal codes, compiled by Rabbi Josef Karo in the sixteenth century.

siman (pl. *simanim*: "sign" or "symbol"): Something that holds symbolic meaning, pointing beyond itself. For example, Rosh HaShanah foods such as apples, honey, and pomegranates, the items on the Pesach seder plate, and the drops of wine spilled during the seder at the recitation of the plagues (spoken according to Rabbi Yehudah's acronym for them: *dalet, tzadi, kaf, ayin, dalet, shin, bet, aleph, chet*).

sinat chinam ("gratuitous hatred"): A term found in Talmud (*Yoma* 9b) attributing the destruction of the Second Temple (70 CE) to the divisive intolerance among Jews of differing groups that prevented them from uniting to deal with the Roman Empire. Gratuitous hatred based on differences is considered a grave sin and is mentioned in the Yom Kippur confessionals.

Sitra Achra (Aramaic, "other side"): In later Jewish mysticism, the dark side of God that accounts for temptation and evil in the world.

Suffering Servant of Isaiah 53: A figure in the book of Isaiah symbolizing the People Israel who suffers because of the actions of others but with God's help is ultimately vindicated and redeemed. These prophecies are of hope and comfort, originally addressed to the Israelites exiled after the Babylonian conquest of Judah, but continually reapplied to Jews suffering at the hands of hostile majority groups.

Tachanun (Supplication): A prayer of penitence and lamentation recited in the daily morning service following the Amidah except on Shabbat, festivals, and during the month of Nisan, the month of redemption in which Pesach occurs.

tallit: A ritual prayer shawl marked with tzitzit, or fringes, on four corners.

tefillin: These ritual objects are worn during daily morning services (not on Shabbat or festivals). Tefillin consist of two small black leather boxes containing excerpts from Exodus 13:1–10 and 11–16 and Deuteronomy 6:4–9 and 11:13–21 written on parchment. Leather straps bind one box to the arm and one to the head. YouTube videos can be accessed that demonstrate how to put on tefillin. Both Sephardic and Ashkenazic traditions exist for how the tefillin are tied.

***Teku* (Hebrew acronym for "let it stand"):** A Talmudic phrase ending a discussion in which the arguments are so perfectly balanced that they cannot be resolved. Traditionally, *Teku* is thought to be an acronym for "The Tishbite [Elijah the Prophet, who will announce the coming of the final redemption] will resolve all challenges and problems."

Tikkun Chatzot: A midnight liturgy recited mainly by mystics. Its themes are mourning the destroyed Temple, the exile of the Jewish people from their land, and estrangement from the Divine. Its two sections, Tikkun Rachel and Tikkun Leah, are addressed to the imminent and transcendent faces of the Shekhinah, the aspect of the Divine that is imaged as feminine.

tohu va-vohu: The primordial chaos preceding the creation of the universe. Colloquially used to mean "a big mess."

Tree of Sefirot: In Kabbalah, the ten attributes through which God manifests in our world are often depicted as constituting a tree. They are the Divine Crown (Keter), Wisdom (Chochmah), Understanding (Binah), Mercy (Chesed), Justice (Din), Beauty (Tiferet), Eternity (Nezach), Glory (Hod), Foundation (Yesod), and God's Presence in the World (Shekhinah). For additional information on tree symbolism in Judaism, see Tu B'Shevat in "The Cycle of the Jewish Year."

tzaddik (m.), tzadeket (f.) (pl. tzaddikim): A righteous or holy person.

unio mystica: In the world of mysticism, the complete union of a mystic's soul with the Divine.

yetzer ha-ra: The impulse to do evil. Every human being possesses both a *yetzer ha-ra* and a *yetzer ha-tov*. To be human is to be a chooser between the two.

yetzer ha-tov: The impulse to do good.

Yom Tov: A Jewish festival. As on Shabbat, Jews are not to engage in specified kinds of work and instead expected to celebrate and pray.

Zohar (Splendor): A primary text of Jewish mysticism, attributed to Shimon bar Yochai but believed to have been written in Spain during the thirteenth century by Moshe ben ShemTov de Leon.

About the Author

R ACHEL A DLER IS THE D AVID E LLENSON Professor of
Modern Jewish Thought at the Hebrew Union College-Jewish
Institute of Religion Los Angeles campus. She pioneered in
integrating feminist perspectives into interpreting Jewish texts
and law. Her book *Engendering Judaism* (1998) is the first by
a female theologian to win a National Jewish Book Award for
Jewish Thought. Rabbi Adler has a doctorate in Religion and
Social Ethics from University of Southern California, rabbinical ordination from Hebrew Union College in 2012, a master of
arts in English literature from Northwestern University, and a
master of social work from University of Minnesota.

She has published over fifty-five articles, many of them
reprinted in collections. Recent articles include "The Torah,
Our Chavruta" in *These Truths We Hold: Judaism in an Age
of "Truthiness,"* edited by Joshua Garroway and Wendy
Zierler (CCAR Press, 2020); "Equality of Social and Political
Rights Irrespective of Sex" in *Deepening the Dialogue: Jewish-
Americans and Israelis Envisioning the Jewish Democratic
State,* edited by Rabbis Stanley M. Davids and John L. Rosove
(CCAR Press, 2019); "For These I Weep: A Theology of Lament"
(*CCAR Journal,* 2014); and "Guardianship of Women in Islamic
and Jewish Legal Texts" with Ayesha Chaudhry in *Islamic and*

Jewish Legal Reasoning: Encountering Our Legal Other edited by Anver Emon (Oneworld, 2017). Books in progress include *Pour Out Your Heart Like Water: Jewish Perspectives on Suffering* (Oxford) and *Gender and Jewish Thought: Theology and Ethics* with Rachel Sabath Beit-Halachmi.